LANGUAGE AND INSIGHT

LANGUAGE AND INSIGHT

The Sigmund Freud Memorial Lectures 1975–1976
University College London

ROY SCHAFER

New Haven and London Yale University Press
1978

Designed by Thos Whitridge
and set in Baskerville type.
Printed in the United States of America by
Vail-Ballou Press, Binghamton, New York.

Published in Great Britain, Europe, Africa, and Asia
(except Japan) by Yale University Press, Ltd.,
London. Distributed in Latin America by Kaiman &
Polon, Inc., New York City; in Australia and New
Zealand by Book & Film Services, Artarmon,
N.S.W., Australia; and in Japan by Harper & Row,
Publishers, Tokyo Office.

Library of Congress Cataloging in Publication Data

Schafer, Roy.
    Language and insight.

    (The Sigmund Freud memorial lectures; 1975–1976)
    Bibliography: p.
    Includes index.
    1. Psychoanalysis—Addresses, essays, lectures.
2. Psycholinguistics—Addresses, essays, lectures.
3. Insight in psychotherapy—Addresses, essays,
lectures. I. Title. II. Series.
RC509.S35   616.8'917   77-20940
ISBN 0-300-02173-9

The author gratefully acknowledges permission by
Random House, Inc., to quote from "In Memory of
Sigmund Freud (d. Sept. 1939)," copyright 1940,
renewed 1968, by W. H. Auden, from *Collected Poems,*
by W. H. Auden, edited by Edward Mendelson.

To
the memory of my wife, Cecily

CONTENTS

PREFACE

Public lectures in a university setting must, it seems to me, do more than give an overview of a subject or build some bridges between the old and the new within a discipline. They must also create their own audience. They must rapidly instruct a group of interested laypersons on selected fundamental concepts, findings, and methods; help them to question the ideas they have just begun to accept and induce them to care about the answers to the questions being raised; and finally, one hopes, convince them of the merits of the types of answers being proposed by the lecturer. No small task! The lecturer may move too quickly for some and too slowly for others, or tread too lightly or too heavily. Undertaking such lectures is, however, a rewarding task. By requiring the speaker to make critical decisions on the strategy of presentation, it forces him or her to clarify the strategy of the discipline that is being discussed. In the present instance, the overriding question becomes, What is psychoanalysis? Although the answer to so large a question must remain schematic and fragmentary in so short a series of lectures, the way in which the answer is being approached may communicate a vision of the discipline as a whole. This at any rate was my hope.

The five lectures that constitute the body of this

book were delivered as public lectures during the fall
and winter of 1975–76 at University College London.
I was then the first Sigmund Freud Memorial Visiting
Professor, occupying a chair established through the
beneficence of the Hon. David Astor. In these lectures
I address some of the most fundamental and problematic issues in the theory, method, and principles of interpretation that constitute the discipline of psychoanalysis: the idea of a psychoanalytic life history; the
meaning and uses of the method of free association;
the concepts of self-control, self-love, and self-hatred;
and the understanding of sexual disorders in relation
to sexist thinking and practices in society. These discussions articulate and extend theses I put forward in *A
New Language for Psychoanalysis,* published by Yale
University Press in 1976.

The Afterword is a revised and expanded version of
an invited presentation of my recent theoretical work
that I made at the fall meeting of the American Psychoanalytic Association in December 1976. Although
written for an audience of psychoanalytic colleagues, it,
too, owing to the novelty of its content, had to meet
many of the requirements of a public lecture. It is included here as a summary of the principal points made
in the longer book and the London lectures.

Throughout these lectures, I emphasize and explore
the essential relations between language, insight, and
the concept of the person as agent. I contrast this
approach with the traditional metapsychological approach, introduced by Freud, which tends to neglect
these relations and to favor instead mechanistic explanations of those profoundly significant human phe-

nomena that are the objects of psychoanalytic investigation. I try to show that what is most characteristic and most valuable about psychoanalysis, and what links it most closely to contemporary thought, becomes apparent through substituting the new language of action for the old one of metapsychology. The future of psychoanalysis rests on its systematic clarification of its own concepts; only in that way can it give the best possible account of what it is to think psychoanalytically. Conceptual transformation goes hand in hand with preservation and enhancement of the good.

The references to the psychoanalytic literature are scanty, and I have entered into the Bibliography only those references that bear in some important way on the arguments being developed. The broad range of references that give the background of my major theses will be found in *A New Language for Psychoanalysis*, where they more properly belong.

New York, New York
March 31, 1977

ACKNOWLEDGMENTS

First and moremost, one must give fullest thanks to Mr. David Astor, benefactor of the Sigmund Freud Memorial Visiting Professorship at University College London.

I also wish to thank the members of the Board of Management of the Freud Professorship for having invited me to be the first to occupy that Chair. The invitation was thrilling and challenging, and my tenure was rewarding in every way. Many on the Board were kind to me during my stay in London: The Provost, Lord Annan, Chairman; Professor George Drew, Head of the Department of Psychology, which Department served as my host; Dr. Christopher Lucas, Director of the Student Health Center, where I was given my place to work; Professor Richard Wollheim, Head of the Department of Philosophy; Miss Marilyn Gallyer, Senior Administrative Assistant; Dr. Alan Tyson; and, of course, Mr. Astor himself. I owe a special debt to Cecily de Monchaux, who at the time was Senior Lecturer in Psychology at University College London and later was to become my wife and a Visiting Lecturer in the Department of Psychiatry of the Cornell University Medical College. She expressed her dedication to psychology, psychoanalysis, and University College London, by helping me in countless ways to give shape

to the new professorship and to bring these lectures to
their final form and publication. A visiting professorship must be a joint enterprise, and whatever degree
of success was achieved in this instance reflects the
gracious support and interest shown by those I have
mentioned as well as by many others at University College London. Thanks are also due to Tom Morawetz,
Department of Philosophy, Yale University, for his
thoughtful critiques of early drafts of these lectures.

The first lecture, "The Psychoanalytic Life History," was my Inaugural Lecture and was published
as a pamphlet for University College London by H. K.
Lewis and Co., London; I am grateful to the Board
of Management for permission to republish it here.
I also wish to thank Random House for permission
to quote, in the Prologue to these lectures, from "In
Memory of Sigmund Freud (d. Sept. 1939)."

LANGUAGE AND INSIGHT

PROLOGUE

In his wartime poem of 1940, "In Memory of Sigmund Freud (d. Sept. 1939)," the late W. H. Auden told how Freud was "taken away"

> *To go back to the earth in London,*
> *An important Jew who died in exile.*

The poet hastened to add this cry of outrage:

> *Only Hate was happy, hoping to augment*
> *His practice now, and his dingy clientele*
> *Who think they can be cured by killing*
> *And covering the gardens with ashes.*

Against the figure of Hate, Auden was holding up the image of Freud's psychoanalysis: it was an image of love and enlightenment in a world overrun with ugliness; of forgiveness, restoration, and reunion; of enthusiasm, delight, and dedication; and of the preciousness of the honestly remembered and individualized life. Perhaps lacking the stern, uncompromising element, but still very true to its subject.

What, then, could be more appropriate than establishing the Freud Memorial Professorship in London? London, too, for its having long been the home and center of creative work of Freud's distinguished daughter, Miss Anna Freud, and of so many other notable and dedicated psychoanalysts. And that this inaugural is taking place at University College London adds all the more to the appropriateness of the occasion, for this college already proudly claims among its many humane and enlightened firsts its taking into its student body Jews, women, and other victims of prejudice —the socially repressed who are the counterparts and often the symbols of the individually repressed. I can imagine no honor greater for a psychoanalyst, and none more moving, than to be chosen to inaugurate this Memorial Professorship.

The Inaugural Lecture
THE PSYCHOANALYTIC LIFE HISTORY

For some years now the chief problem confronting psychoanalytic theoreticians has been the need to develop a new language in which to speak of their methods and findings and conduct their debates with one another and with members of other disciplines. This need has developed as a result of searching and successful critiques of Freud's natural science language—what he called his metapsychology—by psychoanalysts and philosophers. Inevitably, successful critiques leave a void that must be filled. In the instance of psychoanalysis, the void can be filled neither by any ordinary or common-sense locutions nor by impressionistic, idiosyncratic, quasi-poetic rhetoric. Although both sorts of expression constitute the clinical dialogue, just as they make up communication and thought in daily life, they will not serve for systematic discourse. The reason they will not serve is that these languages follow tacit, elusive, and incompatible rules of every kind. They render psychological events both as entities and as processes, the one calling for nominative and adjectival designations and the other for verbal and adverbial designations. In addition, their employment is characterized by frequent switching from the active voice to the passive, from plain description to metaphoric allusion, and from abstract to concrete terms.

What is especially important in this connection is that, when speaking either of these languages, the theoretician and layperson alike typically switch at those points where they encounter either problems of logical consistency or difficulties in thinking through and articulating some ambiguous notion. Or, if not there, then at those points where switching helps modulate or

avoid emotional tension. All of which we can appreciate as conducive to good work, good rapport, and good
spirits, but never as well suited for framing the systematic propositions that constitute a discipline.

With all its imperfections, metapsychology is systematic, and its durability has depended heavily on
this fact. Its constituent terms, such as *energy, force,
structure,* and *mechanism,* imply definite and binding
rules that make possible a high degree of coherence
within and among metapsychological propositions. A
new language for psychoanalysis must do the same.

In deciding on a new language for psychoanalysis,
one must first decide just what kind of discipline clinical psychoanalysis is. It has been becoming increasingly
clear in recent years that clinical psychoanalysis is an
interpretive discipline whose concern it is to construct
life histories of human beings. The principal business
of psychoanalysis is to interpret and reinterpret in life-
historical perspective the verbal and other utterances
of the analysand during the psychoanalytic session.
Psychoanalysis is used to establish meaning or significance where none has been apparent, as in the instance
of seemingly senseless compulsions, and to increase the
intelligibility of its data by establishing the life-historical contexts of that which is to be further understood,
as in the instances of dreams and inhibitions. That its
objects of study—the analysand primarily and the analyst secondarily—are human beings cannot be over-
emphasized. They are persons who have been shaped
by language and who now use it to create new meanings
and so new worlds. In this they are unlike atoms, stars,
acids, bridges, machines, computers, or lower organ-

isms. Consequently, the discipline of psychoanalysis faces problems that are much more like those of the humanities than those of the natural sciences. These are the problems of perspective, subjective evidence and inference, and reliability and validity of interpretation. Specifically, the discipline must develop an ordered account of the doings of human beings in a special kind of relationship into which only language-using, historically oriented human beings can enter—the psychoanalytic relationship.

It was the modern existential and phenomenological thinkers who laid the groundwork for this revised conception of the nature of the psychoanalytic enterprise and who attempted to work out their own humanistic language for psychoanalysis. Their language, or rather their set of overlapping languages, reflects philosophical commitments and projects of many kinds, and, to my way of thinking, it is not well suited to the methods and data of clinical psychoanalysis. This is so perhaps chiefly because these thinkers seem to have used psychoanalysis for philosophical prescription; they have not investigated it as a discipline in its own right.

The project of which I shall speak is that of developing an action language specifically for Freudian psychoanalysis viewed as a life-historical discipline. It is one by means of which psychoanalysts may hope to speak simply, systematically, and nonmechanistically of human activities in general and of the psychoanalytic relationship and its therapeutic effects in particular. The general nature and some of the justification for this language will become evident in the course of this lecture. More will become evident in the lectures to

follow. In executing this project, I have drawn on contemporary philosophical studies of action concepts,
mind, and existence.

I shall be developing three interrelated theses concerning the nature of the clinical psychoanalytic enterprise: that it constructs a personal past of a certain
kind; that it constructs a present subjective world of a
certain kind; and that both of these constructions require a relatively systematic transformation of the
terms in which the analysand defines and understands
his or her life history up to and including the present
moment. I shall be considering only general distin-
guishing features of psychoanalytic interpretation as a
method of history-making and world-defining. It is not
implied that these three theses are the only general
ones that should count in an understanding of psychoanalysis.

Constructing a Personal Past

The first thesis is that a psychoanalysis consists of
the construction of a personal past. It is not *the* personal past but *a* personal past. However convincing it
may be, it remains a construction, merely a history of
a certain kind. To construct any history that is coherent and more than a sprawling and stultifying chroni-
cle, one must lay it out only along certain lines. In
psychoanalytic work, for instance, one is not constructing physiological or narrowly linguistic life histories,
nor is one simply arranging chronologically any kind
of data stated in any kind of terms.

What is distinctive about this Freudian life history?

My answer has two parts: one part concerns that which it is a history of, and the other, which I shall take up in presenting the third thesis, expresses a characteristic point of view we take of this life-historical material. The material itself is organized around personal versions of the major and typical sexual and aggressive conflicts of early childhood. The idea of conflict implies the infantile danger situations, such as loss of loved persons and loss of their love, and the anxieties and defenses that are features of these situations. And the idea of danger situations is conceived subjectively; that is, it refers to children's views of themselves and their worlds, to what they experience emotionally and often unconsciously. Further, one understands each child to be defining this experience largely in the terms of primitive bodily awareness and conceptualization—one might say in terms of infantile categories of understanding. The child's categories are based on organs (mouth, anus, genitalia), substances (feces, urine, milk, blood), movements (sucking, fingering, straining, falling), and contacts (kissing, clinging, hitting). A good case in point is Freud's (1909) obsessional Rat Man of whom one can say this, that unconsciously he was steadily constructing and maintaining a sadistic reality through the application of predominantly anal bodily categories.

In this light Freud's (1923) proposition that the ego is "first and foremost a bodily ego" refers to the formative role played by the categories of psychosexual and aggressive understanding. It is in the terms of these categories that the child constitutes the primitive human reality of the self in its surroundings. The infantile issues of defining oneself and others, of loving and hating oneself and others, of activity and passivity, pleasure and pain, danger, idealization, identification, reparation, reality testing—all of these are constituted in the terms of these categories of understanding. Important as it is to trace the history of these issues throughout the child's development, one must not lose sight of the principle that they are, so to say, authored by the bodily ego. Freud's (1925b) suggestion that the infant's first act of judgment is deciding whether to swallow or spit out implies the oral category of understanding, which, one might add, each of us keeps on using to the last, and not only unconsciously.

This infantile material is not transparent and simply waiting to be organized. For even though the adult analysand may remember some of it in these bodily terms, it is the analyst who starts constituting much of it as analytic data by asking certain questions, following certain methods, and defining only certain contexts of meaning. Undoubtedly, the recovery of unconscious memories and the reconstruction of infantile experience are essential to the method, but one should not confuse this clinical truth with the methodological proposition that the analytic data have to be constituted as such. That proposition says that one cannot establish either the historical sense or the current significance of a fact outside of some context of questions and methods for defining and organizing the material in question. Only by steadily thinking in terms of the infantile, body-based psychosexual and aggressive conflicts can the Freudian analyst define, as psychoanalytically relevant information, what he or she will then use in interpretations.

A complex relation exists between the child's bodily categorial principles and the analyst's organizing concepts. I may have seemed to be contradicting myself, saying on the one hand that the categories are found in the analytic material and on the other hand that they are applied to it by the analyst. To resolve this apparent paradox one must consider another question about the psychoanalytic life history. This is the question whether it is a history that is told forward from its beginning or backward from its ending in the present. It has been said that it is the story of one's life told in reverse and that the method is necessarily retrospective. Although there is much truth in this view of the matter, it does not catch the whole truth. Perhaps the chief point to make against it is that the analyst does not approach each analysis as if having to rediscover psychoanalysis all over again. It is not just that, in all likelihood, the analyst has already taken an anamnesis as part of his or her initial assessment of the analysand's problems and suitability for the psychoanalytic method. More important is the psychoanalytically defined knowledge the analyst already possesses about the typical stages and conflicts of development, the typical modes of moving through these stages and resolving or repressing these conflicts, and the typical ways in which the child's resulting viewpoints on pleasure, danger, failure, and success remain features of adult life.

Here, "typical" includes more than is suggested by the words *normal* or *favorable;* it includes as well many abnormal, traumatic, disruptive features of development, such as severe illness and extreme deprivations. It also includes the disturbing family contexts in which, too often, the formative years are spent, such as cruel

or seductive upbringing, loss of parents or siblings
through death or separation, and radical changes in
physical, social, and emotional milieu. Although psychoanalysts disagree among themselves on the exact nature
and timing of the cognitive and emotional features of
development and on the relative importance of psychic
reality or unconscious fantasy on the one hand and the
actual environment or external reality on the other,
they nevertheless agree on a considerable body of ac-
crued psychoanalytic knowledge about healthy and disturbed development. Psychoanalysts may, on this account, lay some claim to being engaged in a scientific
enterprise: they can say a lot about the conditions or
causes of different types of development. In this respect, psychoanalysis is forword-looking rather than retrospective, developmental rather than historically reconstructive. It remains true, however, that this knowledge of development was in the first instance arrived at
retrospectively or historically; its basic shape has been
not so much altered by the findings of child analysis
and psychoanalytic observation of infants as filled in,
refined, and confirmed by them.

The analyst uses this knowledge, in one or another
of its versions, when listening to the analysand, thinking what that person is likely to have gone through in
order to have arrived at his or her present distinctive
plight. But at the same time the analyst is already conceiving that present plight in terms that reflect the
psychoanalytic account of human development. One
may say that the analyst uses the general past to constitute the individualized present that is to be explained
while using that present as a basis for inquiry into the

individualized past. Thus, while moving with the analysand back and forth through time, the analyst bases
interpretations on both present communication and a
general knowledge of possible and probable pasts that
have yet to be established and detailed in the specific
case.

All of which is to say that for the psychoanalytic life-
historical investigation there is no reverse direction.
The life history, far from being linear or directional, is
circular, for psychoanalytic interpretation is circular.
Events may be recounted forward or backward, but
what counts as an event in this kind of history is established by a circular kind of understanding. Alternatively, interpretation is a particularized creative action
performed within a tradition of procedure and understanding. It has no beginning and no end.

To return now to the question of whether the fateful
bodily categorial principles are found or applied, one
must answer that they are both: the facts are what it is
psychoanalytically meaningful and useful to designate,
and what it is meaningful to designate is established
by the facts; one looks for idiosyncratic versions of what
has usually been found and one finds the sort of thing
that one is looking for. Plenty of room is left for unexpected findings and new puzzles. Like the historian,
the analyst works within this interpretive or hermeneu-
tical circle. Although Freud (1933, p. 121) approached
this point when, in discussing early sexuality, he said
very simply, "Enough can be seen in the children if
one knows how to look," his natural science view of
psychoanalytic investigation prevented him from reaching it.

Constructing a Present Subjective World

What is therapeutic about the construction of this life history, I shall come to later. At this point I want to move on to the second thesis, which is that a psycho-analysis consists of the construction of a present sub-jective world of a certain kind. Again, not *the* present world but *a* present world. Like the past, the psycho-analytic present is no more than one of a number of possible constructions. To be systematic, it must be realized through the consistent application of one set of categories. By this is meant the Freudian present achieved through the Freudian categories.

This present subjective world is not identical with what, in psychoanalytic writing, has been called psychic reality. The concept of psychic reality implies three points: that all the relevant mental processes have al-ready taken place and have organized themselves, un-consciously at least; that this mental activity has been carried on in the very terms of Freudian analysis; and finally, that the business of interpretation is, therefore, simply to uncover hidden ideas or experiences so that the analysand may then deal with them consciously and rationally. I shall bypass the epistemological difficulties of this idea of psychic reality and say only that it does not convey the clinical analyst's interpretive activities accurately or fully. It is not being questioned that psy-choanalysis uncovers already established and uncon-sciously maintained ideas and experiences; nor is it being questioned that this is the case especially for archaic and potentially highly emotional features of existence. It may be accepted that this is the psychic reality the psychoanalyst takes up under the aspects of transference, resistance, and acting out. But with the concept of the present subjective world one is considering the nature of psychoanalytic knowledge itself. And here the point is that the psychoanalyst constructs this world through those aspects of interpretation that implement the Freudian strategy of defining significance, interrelatedness, and context. By means of this strategy one also makes of psychic reality something more than, and something different from, what it has been. Among other things, one establishes for the analysand a perspective on it as primarily a child's atemporal, wishful, and frightened construction of reality, and as such a construction that is in principle modifiable. To accept this modifiability is itself a new action, and one of the most important a person can ever perform.

The psychoanalyst also establishes that the analysand continues to construct this kind of reality out of present circumstance, necessity, and happening. It is only in this connection that one can truly appreciate the importance of constructing the psychoanalytic life history. For, working within the Freudian circle, one cannot investigate and interpret the present subjective world without the understanding to be gained through historical investigation and interpretation. The disturbances of the present life, whether they be symptoms, inhibitions, other functional disruptions, or character malformations, are doomed to remain unintelligible without coordinate historical analysis. The point of the historical inquiry is the elucidation of the present world, especially in its disturbed aspects. The therapist

is not interested in establishing historical explanations
for their own sake; nor is he or she usually preoccupied
with undisturbed functioning, which anyway tends to
remain mostly opaque to psychoanalytic scrutiny. The
therapist aims to be practical, not theoretical. Basically,
he or she is trying to establish the ways in which the
disturbed psychosexual and aggressive past has not yet
become the past. Here one thinks of Freud's (1915)
emphasizing the timelessness of unconscious mental
processes. One wants to establish how the disturbed
past has continued to be, unconsciously, the disturbing
present.

In this way, one gives new meaning and organization
to the disturbing and disturbed present. One wants
especially to show, through what has customarily been
called the analysis of the ego, and of transference, resistance, and acting out, that the analysand's mode of
establishing meaning in the present is based unconsciously on his or her persisting and disturbing application of certain infantile categorial principles. For
example, and here I am speaking schematically, one
wants to show how analysand X repeatedly makes of his
marriage and his analysis the same old painful oedipal
defeat, how Y makes of his masturbation and his psychoanalysis the sadistic activity of his defensive obsessional
regression, and how Z disparages her achievements and
gratifications, both within and outside the psychoanalysis, as her masochistic way of confirming her castrated
status. The analyst is studying the making of psychic
reality as well as the product.

Thus one analyzes the disturbed and disturbing
past-as-the-present and seeks to construct a present that
encompasses the past recognized as such. Here is an

answer to a possible objection that the analysand, after all, comes with a past and a present, though obviously with defective accounts of these. What, it must now be asked, are these defects? How are they to be defined? Are they simply gaps, misrepresentations, and distortions of emphasis? Must one not confront and understand the analysand as defective self-observer as well as defective life-historian, and also as someone who has a desperate interest in blocking or restricting the Freudian type of understanding and who, unconsciously, exercises great skill and perseverance in obscuring, fragmenting, diverting, and otherwise interfering with the psychoanalytic investigation?

The psychoanalyst sees in these defects and strategies the analysand's attempts to achieve and maintain personal discontinuity, both historical and in present psychic reality, and also to impose this discontinuity on others, denying them their own life histories and present worlds. The analysand does not tolerate the idea that the present can only be some comprehensive, even if modified, version of the past—in the end, one hopes, a less fragmented, confining, anguished, and self-destructive modification of that version. Through interpretation, one helps the analysand to abandon the goal of radical discontinuity, of rejection and obliteration of personal pasts and of major features of present existences. It is part of psychoanalytic insight to realize that that goal, which requires a narrow and superficial synthesis at great personal expense, was born of frightening love, hatred, excitement, and depression. At the same time, the psychoanalyst helps the analysand to abandon the goal of thoroughgoing personal continuity, or, in other words, the goal of "cure" without change. The contradictory goals of radical historical discontinuity and total contemporary continuity regularly coexist; this must be so, for they imply each other.

Thus, when psychoanalysts speak of insight, they necessarily imply emotionally experienced transformation of the analysand, not only as life history and present world, but as life-historian and world-maker. It is the analysand's transformation and not his or her intellectual recitation of explanations that demonstrate the attainment of useful insight. The analysand has gained a past history and present world that are more intelligible and tolerable than before, even if still not very enjoyable or tranquil. This past and present are considerably more extensive, cohesive, consistent, humane, and convincingly felt than they were before. But these gains are based as much on knowing *how* as on knowing *that*. Insight is as much a way of looking as it is of seeing anything in particular.

Life History as Action

My third thesis, which concerns the characteristic point of view taken of this distinctively Freudian past and present, is this: the psychoanalyst develops a view of the analysand's life history as action. The term *action* will be used in the sense that includes wishing, imagining, remembering, and other such mental acts along with physical acts in and on the environment. Under *environment* is to be included one's own physical body, for while one acts with this body in many instances, one acts in relation to it as an object as well.

In this comprehensive sense of action, both setting aims and pursuing them are actions; both sitting still and moving are actions; both remembering and repressing are actions. Neurotic symptoms are especially complex actions that simultaneously feature pleasure-seeking, aggression, self-punishment, defense, synthesis, and some adjustment to environmental circumstances in whatever way the analysand views them. To say this is to restate the psychoanalytic principle of multiple function (Waelder, 1930) in the terms of action; that is, it is to give an account in terms of the systems id, ego, and superego, and their mutual relations. On this basis, when patients present symptoms as afflictions or happenings, as by definition they must, psychoanalysts on their part understand them to be disclaiming certain intricate actions that they are performing unconsciously. Other such disclaimings of action include so-called slips, overwhelming impulses, and thoughts that have popped into mind.

In order to speak in terms of action, one must also use the idea of modes of action; for example, there are the modes sadly, impetuously, and curiously. Foremost among the modes of action are the topographic classifications that Freud (1940) finally treated adjectivally, that is, as *qualities* of mental acts, and that, in the design of action language, one must treat adverbially, that is, as *modes* of psychological action. There is no loss of clinical significance in saying *consciously, preconsciously,* and *unconsciously* instead of *conscious, preconscious,* and *unconscious;* there is a gain in theoretical consistency.

One may define any action in multiple ways. The

psychoanalyst regularly establishes that the analysand
has defined certain characteristically disturbing actions
in a number of contradictory ways. In this regard
Freud referred to the tolerance of contradiction in the
system Ucs. or the id. For example, in the choice of a
husband, a woman may, unconsciously, both repudiate
and realize her wish to possess the oedipal father and
in addition may be making a homosexual "object
choice" of a mothering figure. Customarily, the psychoanalyst refers to the multiple definitions of single actions as their overdetermination, even though according to the views now being developed, he or she is referring to meanings rather than causes, and even
though it cannot and need not be demonstrated that
the analysand has been acting in terms of every one of
these meanings, unconsciously or otherwise.

By developing, through interpretation, a conception
of past and continuing life-historical features as actions,
one introduces new and significant actions into the
analysand's history. But one is not necessarily adding
thereby to the explanation of the initial performance of
the actions in question. The point is that psychoanalytic interpretation expands the conception of actions
and that this expansion is an essential constituent of
insight. Insight combines both the old and the new.
The new comprises all those conceptions of life-historical actions, relations, and situations and the analysand
may never before have defined as such.

For example, in repressing and reacting against her
wishing to possess her mother's breast exclusively and
totally, a girl may be performing an action that furthers
the development of an altruistic mode of existence:

there is no absurdity in the psychoanalyst's saying to her
as an adult analysand that this was the course of action
on which she embarked from early on, though at the
time she could not have realized it. Absurdity enters at
the point where one ascribes this retrospective designation of the action to the early infantile mind, as when
one maintains that the very young infant can be so sophisticated as to conceive of altruism, altruistic intentions or motives, or a self that is altruistic. Put in historical perspective, there is far more to an action than
could have entered into its creation at the moment of
its execution. It is the same as the effect of a new and
significant literary work or critical approach on all previous literature: inevitably, fresh possibilities of understanding and creation alter the literary past.

Logically, the idea of multiple and new definitions of
individual actions implies multiple and changeable life
histories and multiple and changeable present subjective worlds for one and the same person. To entertain
this consequence is no more complex an intellectual
job than it is to entertain, as psychoanalysts customarily
do, multiple and changeable determinants and multiple and changeable self- and object representations. Ultimately, of course, the analysand should not be em-
ploying these different perspectives in a way that keeps
them emotionally isolated from one another or forever
in great flux.

The reconceptualization of psychoanalytic theory
and interpretation in the terms of action follows Otto
Fenichel's (1941) technical argument that the analysand must be brought to recognize unconscious defense
as personal activity. In action terms, the scope of dis-

claimed action then shrinks progressively. One sees that this is so upon observing that those analysands who are benefiting from analysis regard and present themselves more and more as the authors or agents of significant factors in their past and present lives and less and less as victims and patients or passive sufferers. They then enter more freely into emotionally interactive personal relationships recognized as such.

To emphasize action is not to deny the place of necessity and accident in the lives of human beings. Through interpretation, analysands get to know, for example, that they have created neither their parents' physical and psychological limitations and excesses nor the traumatic events of their own infancies. Interpretation typically helps them feel less painfully inferior or unworthy because, among other necessities, their parents *could* not love them well, or at all.

These same analysands also get to recognize the extent to which, and the manner in which, they once put certain constructions on infantile events, such as the primal scene, the birth of siblings, weaning, toilet training, anguished losses—and not being well loved. They get to see that, unconsciously, they have been continuing to put the same basic constructions on significant events and relationships in their current lives. And so they come to regard themselves not as helpless objects who have found themselves cut off from large segments of actual or possible pleasure and security by hostile forces, unyielding barriers, or remorseless enemies, but as people who have, for certain reasons, been seeing to it that they remain cut off from these experiences, and who, subtly or crudely, have enlisted others to aid them in this irrational enterprise. Moreover, the others whom they have enlisted exist not only in the present actual world but in the imagined world of inner or surrounding infantile personal relations; indeed, these imagined internal and surrounding presences and interactions are often the most important figures and events of all. I am referring here to such phenomena as the unconsciously imagined presence of the devouring mother, the castrating father, their idealized or damaged breasts, penises, and other organs, and their blows, caresses, and withdrawals.

Thus, in the course of personal transformation, analysands discover, acknowledge, and transcend their infantile categories and their defects as life-historians and world-makers. They see that they have been not the vehicles of a blind repetition compulsion, but the perpetrators of repetition at all costs. They reclaim their disclaimed actions, including their so-called mechanisms of defense, and in so doing, they revise them and are in a position to limit their use of them or in some instances to discontinue using them altogether.

Increasingly, though not of course unfailingly, the analysand and analyst proceed on the strength of a shared recognition that subjective experience itself is a construction. Together, they examine and try to understand the historically founded archaic principles and categories that characterize the analysand's current construction of experience. They no longer think of past or present experience solely or mainly as that which is given and is to be consulted introspectively for clues or answers. Thinking in the new way, they realize that interpretation can only be reinterpretation.

On this basis, the past and the present can be altered radically, and so can the anticipated future.

The psychoanalyst interprets not raw experience, but interpretations. Psychoanalysts imply just this point when they speak of phase-specificity, for they use this term to refer to two things: the child's construction, out of whatever was given at the time, of infantile versions of reality, and their own psychoanalytic reinterpretation of that infantile construction. In this view, and contrary to the common criticism, it is the analysands, not their analysts, who are the reductionists; it is the analysands who repeatedly make of the world a toilet, a spanking, a brothel, a cold breast, or any of the other scenes, objects, or interactions with which psychoanalysts regularly concern themselves. Through life-historical interpretation, the psychoanalyst both defines this reductionism and establishes a perspective on it that curtails its scope and urgency.

There is a special advantage to be gained from viewing the changes facilitated by psychoanalytic therapy as the extension and stabilization of the analysand's commitment to personal agency. In taking this view, one is better able to frame an answer to the question of what difference it makes to become conscious of so many disturbing and hitherto unconscious conflicts or, as it would now be preferable to say, to consider consciously those paradoxical actions that previously one had performed unconsciously, repetitively, and in utter futility. In another form, this question asks how anything is changed, or changed for the better, by the construction of a Freudian life history and present subjective world.

To develop an answer, one must bear in mind that these constructions both presuppose and further the process of changing the analysand's point of view of himself or herself in relation to others; that is to say, in the interpretive circle, the significant observations, memories, insights, and modes of feeling that are made possible by the Freudian constructions also document and extend these very constructions. Under the influence of the psychoanalytic perspective, the analysand not only begins to live in another world but learns how to go on constructing it. It is a transformed world, a world with systematically interrelated vantage points or rules of understanding. It is a world of greater personal authority and acknowledged responsibility. It is more coherent and includes a greater range of constructed experience. It is more socialized and intelligible. At its best it has nothing to do with Freudian jargon, social complacency, or conformity.

And *that* is the difference it makes! For whoever skeptically questions what difference it makes to confront conflicts consciously is presupposing a static reality, an unalterable personal history and world, a life that allows only one interpretation and requires simple either-or choices. That skeptic is also presupposing a subject who cannot be the agent of his or her own experience and life situation, and who at best can be no more than a recaller or witness of happenings and impersonal inner conflicting forces in a fixed reality, a creature inhabiting a world in which one is fated to be without personal authority or responsibility and so, in an ultimate sense, must be passive and existentially incoherent. On that basis, "making the unconscious conscious," if it were possible at all, could only lead to extreme situations—chaos, orgy, panic, mayhem, and self-destruction. But to the extent that the Freudian analysand is learning, devising, and following new rules of understanding, he or she is no longer exactly the same person with respect to whom insight was to be developed; and he or she is no longer creating exactly the same set of desperate situations that were to be rendered intelligible. The person, the reality, the analytic situation, all are correlatives, and all are constantly in flux. Increased intelligibility of persons and situations implies the transformation of agents and their situations.

The Freudian idea of the primacy of person-as-agent does not indict or preclude passive modes of experience with their frequently pleasurable, restorative, and otherwise adaptive aspects. The distinguished psychoanalytic theoretician, Heinz Hartmann (1939), with reference to certain forms of personal rigidity, emphasized the adaptive significance of the ability to yield to biological automatisms, as in the instance of the sexual climax. But this yielding is now to be seen as an action; far from being inactivity, it is something one does. Not everyone does it, at least not always and not in every respect. While it is of some interest to note that this sort of yielding entails refraining from doing other actions, specifically those actions that would block the automatism, it is also to be remarked that we must designate refraining itself an action. In the same way, we must designate as actions delaying, regulating, choosing, and other members of that family of words. Choice or choosing is not a prerequisite of action; it is a form of action. And refraining from interfering is one kind of refraining action, as psychoanalysts know all too well from the method they usually follow in their work.

As much as by its basic categories of past and present life-history and experience, Freudian interpretation is distinguished by its conception of personal existence as actions with multiple and transformable meanings.

The terms of a theory should be wedded to the methods that generate its data. On this basis one may claim that it is the language of action rather than mechanism that is the natural, sufficient, and parsimonious expression of the psychoanalytic method. The terms or rules of action suit a life-historical discipline as the terms of metapsychology do not, for clinical psychoanalysis never has been and never could be a laboratory science dealing in mindless objects and experimentally controlled processes. Psychoanalysis suffers no loss of dignity on this account, and the vast and consequential discoveries that testify to Freud's genius are preserved intact, if not seen in a clearer light. Indeed, in a further unification of one's thinking, one will, as psychoanalyst, now be regarding the analysand's activities just as one regards one's own: not as the resultants of the operation of the functions, energies, forces, and structures of a mental apparatus, but as meaningful and complex actions taken by a person who simultaneously finds and makes a world in which to act. So construed, this is a person who can to a considerable degree remake and refresh that world, both as it is and as it was in the infantile past. And this is the theme of Auden's homage to Freud.

The Second Lecture
FREE ASSOCIATION

In the course of free-associating during a psychoanalytic session an analysand said, "I was promiscuous as a child—*promiscuous* is not the right word—I was hunting for *precocious*." Was he hunting for anything? If not, what was he trying to say by this locution? And how are we to understand or talk about the event of saying the "wrong" word? I call this event a *word-surprise*.

Here are some related examples. "I saw those two black people—I was going to say *Negroes* but that's a word I don't use anymore." "I was going to say *stunned* but I don't think I was." "Then I would be perfect again. Why did I say *again?*" "The sex I had last night was very good—I was going to say the sex I was *getting away with*." "I am afraid of being accused of being an expert—*accused* is not the word for it; I don't know why I said it." "The word *despise* comes to mind but that's not how I think you feel about me." Each such statement seems to presuppose a number of things about the nature of doing, thinking, and saying, and thus to imply some theory of mind or self that is not in accord with the troublesome locution and so has occasioned surprise.

With less sense of discordance and surprise, or perhaps none at all, analysands will say such things as the following. "The thought of my father crossed my mind." "The word *unfaithful* popped into mind." "My thoughts are rattling around." "Nothing at all comes to mind." "The idea of revenge suggests itself." "That idea makes me think of my troubles with my professor." I designate this class of locutions *disclaimed actions*. They are instances of mental action or other

action that the speakers are disavowing by treating
them as happenings, that is, as events in the coming
about of which they, as agents, have played no part.
The idea of disclaimed action, to which I shall return,
applies to much of the material presented in my discussion of free association below.

The class of locutions that are discordant and occasion surprise poses fundamental problems: specifically,
for psychoanalysts' theory of free association, and generally, for their theory of mentational activity. For this
reason I make it my chief point of reference in this
lecture and, in another way, in the next. The problems are those entailed by the way psychoanalysts answer two questions: "What is it to think or say the
'wrong' word?" and "How do we ever get to say or
think anything?" However, in order to tackle these
questions, I must first spend some time picturing
the free-association method on which psychoanalysis
depends.

Free Association

The method of free association is also referred to as
the fundamental rule of psychoanalysis. According to
this rule, the analysand agrees to suspend so far as
possible his or her ordinary standards of verbal reasonableness, coherence, and decorum, and simply report
freely to the analyst whatever is thought or experienced
at the moment. The analyst, it is stated or implied,
will not judge or otherwise react personally to what is
reported, but rather will attempt to use the associations
to unravel the mysteries of the analysand's problems,

whether they be symptoms, inhibitions, painful moods, anxiety states, or whatever. Although psychoanalysts vary in the way in which they introduce this rule, in the time at which they do so, and in the insistance with which they call attention to its evident violations—who can ever speak that freely for any period of time?— they more or less follow Freud's model: they introduce the rule at the very beginning, they explain it as a matter of saying whatever comes to mind or whatever one can observe introspectively, and from then on they dose and temper their vigilant reminders with tact and with best guesses as to when it will be useful to point out, question, or interpret violations of the rule.

The fundamental rule is pressed into further service. When something is mentioned that seems both unintelligible or not yet sufficiently understood and indicative of important personal issues, the analyst may ask the analysand to associate to it specifically. It may be a dream as a whole or the details of a dream, a slip of the tongue, a memory, or a symptomatic action such as hurting oneself, dropping something, or showing up late. Thus the analyst might ask the first analysand mentioned above to associate to the word *promiscuous,* and ask the others to associate to the words *Negroes, stunned, perfect again, getting away with* sex, *accused,* and *despise.* Or the analyst might simply listen to the associations that follow each such event, doing so on the assumption that these associations will in some important sense have some bearing on the surprising words or the unintelligible dream, slip, etc.

Psychoanalysts regard the sequence of associations as a route that will have to be traversed in order to reach some revealing end point, say, an important childhood memory or a distressing feeling that has not yet been expressed. But they do not see this as the only possible culmination of the sequence, even though they regard it as one major possibility. Analysts listen to associations in two other main ways.

One way is to attempt a thematic analysis of the various ideas and feelings that the analysand is expressing. The analyst attempts a contextual analysis of the associations. There are some now who compare this way of listening to text analysis, though they do not seem to take into account that the listening and the interpreting play a major part in the further development of the text that is being analyzed. Consider the instance of a female analysand associating to a dream image of a wilted flower: she thinks of missed opportunities, the ravages of aging, being unattractive, how things just have to be looked after, and then restlessly and somewhat irritably wonders what the analyst makes of all this. One of the things the analyst makes of all this, through thematic or contextual analysis, is that the analysand feels unappreciated, unhelped, neglected, and deprived in relation to the analyst, and that she is implying that some romantic interest on his part might make or keep things beautiful. And since this theme or context is discerned in the more general context of her unrequited love for her father—the dream and the associations having been reported during a period when this unrequited love has evidently been a recurrent theme—an analyst also infers that the same mixture of longing and recrimination directed toward the father is now being directed toward him: it is he, now, who is not helping her bloom into sexual womanhood. (Perhaps as well, though at the moment it might not be to the point to mention it, he is not feeding her as a good mother would.) Though this example is schematic and incomplete, it does illustrate thematic or contextual transference interpretation of the dream and the free associations to it. When one is listening in this way, in a context of understanding, an end point is not in question.

The third way in which analysts listen to associations is by attempting to infer disturbing content from the form or style of the associations. The very activity of associating, of producing associations, of discoursing aloud no matter what, is from the first viewed by the analysand in terms of personal issues of lifelong emotional importance. For instance, the analysand may view this activity as a way of being a good child in order to please Mother or Father; pressing the analysis further, the analysand may be viewing being a good child as, to give only two examples, always meeting the demands of others and expressing no needs of one's own, or being a clean and dutiful child who does what is required expeditiously. In the first of these two instances, further analysis may reveal that this way of dealing with demands and one's own needs implies a strategy of uncomplaining submission to weaning and an unenvious attitude toward younger siblings being nursed; in the second instance, the further implication may be that of submitting obediently to strict toilet training. In the first instance the associations themselves, apart from their content, will have the significance of milk, feeding, and the denial of craving;

in the second instance, the associations will be experienced as feces. In either instance the analyst might interpret the analysand's unswerving dedication to producing associations, or his or her responding anxiously to seeming to have little to say, as evidence that one of these parts is being played. In the same vein, the analyst might interpret the suspension of associations as some form of oral demand or anal rebellion.

In the majority of instances, the analyst's thematic or contextual analysis of the content of the associations will support these interpretations of form or style, so that it will not be a matter of the analyst's making clever guesses based on only one kind of evidence; rather it will be a matter of everything pointing to the interpretation—the allusiveness of the starting point and end point, the contextual perspective on content, and the form or style of the associative process. It may require a stretch of time before any interpretation can be arrived at, and when it does take form it may have to be set in a still larger context or linked with other contexts in order that some more encompassing and articulated insight may be aimed at; for example, the oral and anal issues may finally be viewed as defensive regressions from oedipal issues.

To give a more concrete example: one analysand with marked obsessive-compulsive problems, based as is usually the case on an unconsciously maintained anal orientation to himself and his world, would at times grunt, groan, and writhe on the analytic couch in his efforts to force out some of his thoughts and feelings; finally he would appeal to the analyst explicitly for help in "getting it out." Upon analysis, this conduct proved to be a reenactment of his ambivalence during and after toilet training with respect to holding on to or letting go of his stools; it was also a reenactment of his conflictual retentive-expulsive actions in other areas of his life. In his childhood he often had ended up requiring help from his mother in completing his evacuations. It also emerged that he derived some secret masturbatory pleasure from the considerable and prolonged anal stimulation occasioned by his intermediate "paralysis."

Here is another example: This analysand unconsciously equated the fundamental rule with the rigid, perfectionistic demands his mother had made during his early years. Uncompromisingly and prematurely, she had wanted him to be self-sufficient and to maintain a controlled, proper, and pleasing appearance. To this tyranny he had submitted superficially while finding innumerable covert ways of resisting it. To complicate matters, his mother, who prided herself on her good looks as well as her iron control, was also significantly seductive in her relationship with him, so that he experienced being both strongly enticed and encouraged to be seductive himself while yet remaining caged up by her. He reenacted this dilemma in his orientation toward the fundamental rule, viewing it as one calculated simultaneously to overexcite and confine him. He manifested this view by his way of associating and his way of viewing the analytic relationship generally, for these displayed the same configuration of superficial submission, covert rebellion, seductiveness, flight from seduction, and imprisonment. He continued this repetition or re-creation over a long stretch of time

when the manifest material he was bringing up was of
every different kind. The content of his associations
only began to correspond to the form or style of his
analytic conduct as interpretation progressively established that he was indeed acting that way, and that he
was doing so not only in the analysis but, chronically,
in his extra-analytic relationships as well.

The interpretations just mentioned are certainly not
complete interpretations; matters were far more complex than that. They do, however, illustrate my point
about interpreting form or style as content and doing
so in conjunction with sequences and contexts of association. Interpreting form or style as content is essential in bringing about emotionally experienced insight
and personal transformation through psychoanalysis;
without it, all other interpretation tends to remain
merely interesting, perhaps plausible, speculation.

The Complexity of the Analytic Dialogue

I want to explore next the working assumption that,
however different things may appear, the analysand is
always speaking to the analyst. Associating in the analytic situation is necessarily a relational activity. In
addition, more than two people are involved in the dialogue; the two-person analytic relationship is, in fact, a
crowd. The analysand is also speaking to imagined
presences or internal figures representing significant
people who have been important in his or her past,
and at different times he or she is speaking to the analyst as a representative of one or another of these significant figures. Also, the analysand receives the ana-

lyst's interpretations within this fantasized framework; that is, the analysand takes them as personal, probably familial interventions. Consequently the phases and facets of the analytic relationship, usually subsumed under the terms *transference* and *resistance,* are constant reference points for interpretation. The notion that psychoanalysis is some kind of detached and impersonal undertaking whereby the analysand produces evidence in the form of associations and the analyst figures out their meaning and gives the answer is an idea that corresponds only to certain defensive fantasies entertained by some people in analysis and by some of those thinking about analysis from the outside.

A final point to be made in this connection is this: it is the analyst as well as the analysand who may unconsciously attribute familial significance to the analytic working relationship. In the analyst's case, these attributions are subsumed under the term *countertransference.* It is assumed that under ordinary conditions countertransferences do not significantly or lastingly disrupt the analytic work. In fact, they may enhance rather than disrupt that work, for in many instances they may rightly be taken as the first recognizable signs that some as yet undefined and pressing problems of the analysand are affecting the analyst's orientation to the working relationship.

Is "Free Association" the Right Name for It?

I go on now to call your attention to two assumptions underlying the usual psychoanalytic approach to free association. The first assumption is that it is not *free,*

and the second is that it is not *association*. At least it is
not merely free and not merely association. Freud assumed that everything the analysand does is strictly
determined, especially by unconscious forces. From this
perspective, the point of the free-association method
is to make it plain just how unfree the analysand is. In
this connection the designation "free" makes sense
only as referring to one's freeing oneself from the usual
self-imposed constraints of verbal reasonableness, coherence, and verbal decorum. But even this freedom
is illusory, for under the aspect of resistance or defense
it soon becomes apparent that, as Edward Glover (1955,
p. 27) once remarked, following the introduction of
the fundamental rule the remainder of the analysis consists in the analysand's efforts to circumvent it. In short,
in the analytic relationship nothing that counts is free.
The suggestion that it is free establishes the associations
as disclaimed actions; on this basis the analysand is
helped to bring up all sorts of matters in all sorts of
ways with less sense of responsibility and danger than
would be felt otherwise, and in the long run this help
has its advantages.

Turning next to the "association" half of free association, one must first ask just what kind of theory of
mentation Freud was using. It was not fundamentally
the associationistic theory of the academic psychology
that prevailed in his day. According to that theory,
factors such as primacy, recency, contiguity, and frequency of occurrence determine the linear sequence of
thoughts, arranging them like links in a chain. One
does observe phenomena that suggest the play of such
factors, and in his explanatory propositions Freud did

seem to include these factors and the mental model they implied. But for the most part his making that inclusion played a superficial or incidental role in his explanations. What was primary for Freud was the organizing influence of unconscious conflict in which infantile wishes and fears figure decisively. These are the unconscious forces or determinants acting like magnets organizing iron filings in their magnetic fields. And this in effect is the idea of thematic or contextual analysis expressed by way of a physicalistic metaphor. Analysands may seem to be talking about all kinds of things; analysts, while recognizing the superficial associative links, center their attention on defining the contexts and the interrelations of the associations' meanings. The analyst's assumption is this: at any given phase of the analytic work, only superficially is it possible for the analysand to talk about all kinds of things; the analysand cannot even manage to change the subject, for at the least trying to do so amounts to saying, *"This,* I don't want to talk about"; and more often than not, once the analyst is familiar enough with the analysand, he or she will be able to discern in the apparent change of subject a continuation of the troublesome theme in another guise or else the introduction of another facet of that very theme.

A comparable case is encountered in the relation of the manifest dream content to the latent dream thoughts. The disparate or incoherent features of the manifest dream, which seem to lead everywhere and nowhere, prove on analysis to be archaic, iconic ways of saying some important things about one's present life situation and its infantile prototypes. Once it is

understood, the dream is a coherent, sensible statement even if predicated on some fantastic infantile
assumptions.

In his comments on free association in his conversations on Freud (1942, p. 42), Wittgenstein seemed to
miss the mark when he raised the following question:
"But this procedure of free association and so on is
queer, because Freud never shows how we know where
to stop—where is the right solution?" Wittgenstein assumed that the game being played is simply the linear,
associationist, and detached puzzle-solving game of free
association. He did not realize that the associations,
both in their form and content, end—they may even
be interrupted!—when an interpretation becomes possible and the analysand's going on talking would be
beside the point of immediate concern. This is the
point where an explicit analytic dialogue is indicated.
There are contextual rules of various sorts for deciding
when that point has been reached. Learning how to do
analysis entails learning these rules. In fairness to Wittgenstein, it should be pointed out that he did go on
to say, "When a dream is interpreted, we might say it
is fitted into a context in which it ceases to be puzzling"
(p. 45). But this was the main thrust of Freud's argument, obscured perhaps by his mechanistic and associationist terms. Wittgenstein's further remarks on re-
dreaming the dream in the course of telling it and
associating to it, and on the questions of evidence and
whether dreams qualify as a kind of language, suggest
many fruitful lines of discussion that cannot be pur-
sued here.

Word-surprises and Action

In one form or another, the traditional metapsychological explanation of the surprising locutions I call
word-surprises would invoke the idea of unconscious
wishes, impulses, or motivations. These factors would
be assigned to the id, the superego, and the defensive
portions of the ego, and one would speak of them as in-
vading, disrupting, or taking command of the apparatus of speech or some of the ego functions involved in
thinking and speaking. It would be supposed that these
dynamic factors lie in wait for opportunities to express
themselves. What I want to emphasize about this account is not its odd and untenable mixture of mechanism and anthropomorphism, nor do I want to show
that this mixture is an inescapable feature of metapsychology; I and others have attempted that job elsewhere (see, e.g., Klein, 1976; Holt, 1976; Schafer,
1976), and it would lead too far afield to dwell on it
here. I do want to emphasize two other important considerations: the disclaiming of action entailed in this
way of thinking and the distance of this explanation
from the actual nature of clinical interpretation.

The motivational or psychodynamic account in question entails disclaimed action in this way: it says that
forces are acting on ego functions so as to disrupt or
subvert them, and that the only agency involved in the
event is the impersonally and biologically conceived
ego. The saboteurs of speech are themselves impersonal, being presented under the aspect of causes, and

they are causes that are knowable only indirectly through their manifestations.

The distance of the metapsychological account from clinical interpretation becomes evident when one considers that the analyst might say, in one of my initial examples, "If the word *despise* is what you think of, you must be thinking that in some sense I do despise you, even though you reject the idea that this is so." Of course, the analyst might speak metaphorically, perhaps in the same way as the analysand, and say something like, "If the word *despise* pops into mind . . ." or the analyst might speak deterministically and say, "Something must have caused you to say *despise*." But in whichever vein and with whichever words, the analyst would be making the point that it is not that something has happened to the analysand's thinking but that the analysand has done something—said something—for which he or she cannot at the moment account and moreover is averse to scrutinizing further. The analyst would be suggesting as well that the immediate situation that the analysand has been consciously defining cannot account for the saying of *despise* while another situation could account for this action; furthermore, this other situation must be ominous in some way, seeing that it has to be disavowed. Saying *despise* in this disavowed and ominous situation makes sense, as does fearing to say *despise* outright and only introducing it in the guise of inadvertence. The analyst's position (not his wording) in interpretation, then, is this: "If you said it, you meant it, even though it was not all you meant"; and this position implies that the analysand is in a far more complex situation and is engaged in far more complex actions and acting more conflictually and apprehensively than he or she dares to recognize.

What I am saying is congruent with what Freud (1925a) said on the question of responsibility for one's dreams. Who else, he asked, dreamed the dream? In other words, Freud took the position that a dream is a mental act like any other and that attributions of responsibility for mental acts must be made across the board. In this view, responsibility emerges as a defining feature or constituent element of mental acts and not as a logically independent causal factor. I know I am saying more than Freud said and that I am saying it in another way, but I do not think I am distorting the logical implications of what he said or what any analyst says when making clinical interpretations of free associations, *whatever the wording used.*

What I am saying is also congruent with Freud's (1925b) views on negations, that is, those instances where the first association says what is not the case: for example, "That woman in the dream doesn't remind me of my mother." Freud treated these negations as disguised affirmations. His having done so implied the same logical structure that I have just described. Accordingly, the analyst might say in one way or another, "You did think of your mother after all: you meant it and feared it, and so you had to disclaim it."

In the interpretation the analyst is saying something that has this logical structure: "You have just done *this* in *that* situation." This designation—or redesignation or translation—*is* the interpretation, though perhaps only a fragment of a larger interpretation. In the way the analyst designates the action and the situation, he or she says or implies why it was done. The designation of the action points to the reasons for the doing of the action.

Those analysts who prefer to speak of interpretation as the uncovering or putting into words of unconscious fantasies are, in effect, making the same point. Logically, they are saying something like this: "At the same time as you think you are saying A in situation B, you are also unconsciously saying C in situation D: that is the sense in your saying the 'wrong' word. It is not the wrong word at all, but rather the right word according to your unconscious fantasy. But because the fantasy is unconscious, you are surprised." They are also saying this: "Even your thinking of the 'wrong' word as something that happened to you shows that, unconsciously, you imagine yourself acting as a crippled or helpless person in a threatening situation, a passive victim of alien forces or beings who have seized control of your mind or your speech apparatus." (Again, I am spelling out the logical implications of the interpretation in the terms of unconscious fantasy; I am not suggesting that my way of putting it corresponds exactly to any analyst's manner of wording interpretations.)

Models of Mentation

Thus far there would seem to be no difference in principle between ordinary disclaimers, such as "that popped into mind," and word-surprises, such as *"accused* is not the word for it." But as I forecast earlier, there are some special problems to take up in connection with word-surprises. These are problems connected with tacit models of mentation and its relation to motivation, which I address in the next lecture.

A well-established presupposition, common to both ordinary language and metapsychology, is the notion that we have to think something before we can say it, that somehow we have to prepare it mentally before it is accessible as a statement of some kind. According to this presupposition, it is not credible that, when speaking in our usual manner, we might just be saying whatever it is we do say, or it is not acceptable to say no more than this about much of our discourse. Freud (1915) used this presupposition in formulating his metapsychology. He did so by introducing the assumption that, initially, a thought is unconscious or perhaps preconscious and that it becomes conscious either through a special mental act, which he designated allocating attention cathexis to it, or by its commandeering that cathexis by its very urgency, an urgency derived from its closeness to the drives. This assumption says that we first have to think something before we can know, if we ever do know, that we are thinking it or have thought it. A necessary temporal sequence is being assumed. The illustration with which I began this lecture seems to be in accord with Freud's assumption. You will recall that the analysand said, "I was promiscuous as a child—*promiscuous* is not the right word —I was hunting for *precocious.*" If he was hunting for *precocious,* then he would seem to have already thought of *precocious:* on what other basis could he have been hunting for that very word? I raised the question initially whether he was in fact hunting for anything, and, if not, I asked, what was he trying to say by that locution?

Thinking and speaking are actions. Ordinarily we create or fashion them and take responsibility for them, just as we do in the case of our physical actions in or on the environment, that is, our public behavior. Although thought and action are commonly considered to be two different things, in the most general sense they may be classed together as actions; some writers on action theory have classed them just this way. Speaking is more easily classed as an action than thinking, but if we take thinking as silent speech, as Ryle (1949) proposed, we may view thinking as a private speech-action. Or since it is sometimes possible to infer what someone else is thinking, we may view thinking as an action that ordinarily is private.

I make the point that thinking, speaking, and behaving are actions, in order to pave the way to raising a general question about actions of any sort: whether we must believe that an action has to be prepared before it can be performed. But this question must be wrongly conceived, for wouldn't the preparation of the action be an action, too? It couldn't be a happening. And would that preparation in turn have to be prepared, and if so what about the preparation of that pre-preparation? We encounter here an infinite regress, from which one might conclude that something is wrong with the terms or presuppositions of the argument. I think that this conclusion is correct, and that what is being overlooked is that the concept of action requires us to regard each action as inherently spontaneous, as starting from itself. Of course, many of the things that we say or otherwise do publicly we have constituted during some private period of mental preparation; this is what Freud called experimental action in thought. Planning a project and then executing it is a case in point. But, as I said, private preparation or planning qualifies as action, too, and just where would it start? It is in this sense that we are logically required to regard each action as starting from itself. Actions initiated unconsciously also start from themselves: I am not ignoring this class of actions, nor am I minimizing its importance.

To say that actions start from themselves is not to deny the life-historical methodology of clinical psychoanalysis described in the first lecture; nor is it to deny that actions take place and derive their sense from their contexts. I shall return to this point.

How does this much of the argument bear on the notion of free association? We must now say that a free association is a thought-action that starts from itself. Neither the fact that some associations are temporarily kept private, nor the fact that some are revised by the analysand before being said aloud, has any bearing on the logical point being made. Consequently, the fundamental rule amounts to the analysand's agreeing to speak with as little delay, screening, selection, or revision as possible. The analysand is not agreeing to say what comes to mind, what is brought to mind, what occurs to one, or introspectively to report what goes on in the theater of the mind on the assumption that that is how the mind works or that that is a true rendition of what thinking and reporting is about. It is true that

analysands do report in the introspective mode, but
now we would say that in doing so they can only be
delaying or avoiding speaking freely. It is also true that
it is only by seeming to proceed in this introspective,
delaying mode, at least a good deal of the time, that
people can go through the arduous process of psychoanalysis. Like the previously mentioned disclaimers introduced into the conception of free association, the
"introspective mode'" is a source of security in com-
municating. But neither of these considerations bears
on the question, which is a question in philosophical
psychology or psychology of mind. The question is
whether we are obliged to assume, with Freud, that
what is thought and said must first have been prepared
somewhere and somehow out of awareness in the mental apparatus. The answer is, No, we are not so obliged.

I think Freud (1940) took a step in the direction of
this general discussion when he decided to give up the
designations *unconscious, preconscious,* and *conscious*
as referring to topographic systems of the mind and to
use these terms to refer to "mental qualities." By taking
that step he prepared the way for viewing actions—
including thought-actions—as being performed in different modes and according to different rules, specifically the modes unconsciously, preconsciously, and
consciously and the rules that characterize them. The
central interest of clinical psychoanalysis remains
what it has always been: the analysand's conflictual
mode of acting unconsciously in correlative situations
that have been defined unconsciously at different points
in development. What is changed by the argument I
have been advancing is this: one can now speak more

clearly, more modestly, and more coherently about
the psychoanalytic method and the data it generates
through the rule of free association, so-called.

Associating as Rule-following

To say that the association originates in itself is not
to deny that it is made in a context or a situation. The
association figures as one of the things that that person
would say or think in that situation, whatever it is. In
this respect free associating is a case of rule-following.
It is not that associating is an action obeying a rule that
exists independently of it and prior to it. Rather, free
associating is a ruled or regimented action, as actions
must be by definition; otherwise, associating would be
a case of irremediable incoherence rather than an analytic performance. An association's coming into existence also modifies its situation, if only by filling it in
further, so that one is dealing always with constantly
changing situations. Frequently, the association indicates that the situation is more complex than has so far
been recognized; by so doing, it reconstitutes that situation. For example, the association may show that in
some sense the analytic situation is a danger situation
(e.g., being despised), and once that is recognized, the
analytic context can no longer be quite the same.

It follows from this that agreeing to follow the fundamental rule establishes, from that moment on, not a
stereotyped but a creative self-presentational situation.
That this is so is evident from the fact that once analysands begin free associating, they do all kinds of things
in all kinds of ways. There are innumerable questions

they must answer for themselves. Shall I fill in the previous telling of my life history, and if so, just how?
Shall I describe more about my present life, and if so,
just how? Shall I tell more about what I am like, what
I hope, what the analyst must fear? How is one to go
about it? Is it all right to say anything? Which anything?
Even if the analysand begins with a rehearsed account,
he or she has performed a creative self-presentational
action: it may be one that conveys a fear of spontaneity,
a transference enactment of doing an orderly or clean
job, or whatever. Alternatively, the analysand may
come in with a topic to talk about. But why that topic,
and just how is that topic being talked about, and what
does talking *about* something signify in contrast to talking freely to the analyst and finding out what one will
say (as one gets to do more and more as the analysis
progresses)? Is talking about something a way of
speaking at arm's length? Is it taking the limited part
of an observer-collaborator? Is it a way of controlling
what will take place, trying to make sure there will be
no surprises and thus no independently existing analyst
and no greater complexity to anticipate than one is
already consciously prepared for?

The analyst observes these creative actions which
state or imply definition of self and other in relationship, and makes surmises about the rules the analysand
is following, the situations that are implied by these
rules, and the conflictual historical antecedents and
prototypes that may be the background of this conduct. The analyst listens particularly to the wording of
what is said. For example, a female analysand, speaking
of her husband, says the following to her male analyst:

"I never could love him." The analyst may wonder whether she is indicating a fear that she can't love him, her analyst, or that she does love him but it trying to deny it just as she has denied her loving her husband, and perhaps, before her husband, her father or mother or both; or perhaps she is indicating that as an unloving person she is not lovable. The analyst may wonder why she says "could": Had she been *trying?* Does she thing love is something one accomplishes as a task? Is loving a *can* and *can't* in her world, that is, an ability word? If so, it would suggest that, unconsciously, loving is for her a matter of meeting some kind of oral, anal, or genital demand, or some superego demand, or some combination of such demands.

In studying free-associating as a complex action, the analyst is attempting to define the rules of the analysand's analytic game at that moment. I say "at that moment" because being in analysis is always a complex game in which the rules are constantly changed by the analysand and in which only some of the rules are consciously statable and many are paradoxical. For example, one analysand comes late to his appointment and declares that he does not want to talk about or analyze his lateness. The analyst must in some form wonder, "What can lateness—and especially this instance of lateness—mean to him that he does not want to talk about it? What situation is he in that he might have arranged to be late and then not want to examine this action? What rules is he following at this point? And why at this point and not last week, when he was also late?"

Although the game is complex, the analyst usually is able to ascertain after a while that a specific analy-

sand will repeatedly follow only a limited number of
major and problematic rules; in time the analyst will
also ascertain that the analysand changes these rules in
typical ways and at typical times. One analysand reflected, "I make it a rule in the analysis not to ask
questions, but I guess it's a rule of my life that I bring
into the analysis: I import it." On another occasion the
same analysand said, "I am saying whatever comes into
my mind, but it's a way of arranging it so that it is
mediated by unnecessary concern with detail and lacks
spontaneity." He had come to this realization after the
analyst had commented on his becoming circumstantial
every time he approached a topic that was for him
laden with emotion, as though the circumstantiality
slowed down the pace, put off the emotional moment,
reassured him about his being in control, and protected
him from becoming dangerously emotional in front of
the analyst.

Thus the analyst is in effect always asking, "What is
this analysand doing now? What is the best way to
designate it and the situation it implies?" In particular,
this is how the analyst approaches the word-surprise.

The genius of the free-association method lies not in
its establishing suspension of rules but in its making
plain the rules embodied in the analysand's associating.
Thereby it makes plain the complexity of the analysand's actions and the situations corresponding to these
actions. Analysands frequently become aware of this
contribution of the free-association method when they
discover, usually with the help of interpretation, that
they are imposing rules, such as that one is not to ask
questions or say another word once the analyst calls

time. But the more important insight they achieve is this, that however they act, they cannot do otherwise than perform ruled actions, and that the crux of analysis is the definition of these rules and the tracing of the history of these rules, especially the more disruptive ones: What is forbidden to think? What must one do to atone sufficiently? What is the way to get gratification in disguise, and why that disguise, and why any disguise? What is to be renounced and why and since when? These are questions about rules. They are questions that come up through examination of the ruled nature of the allegedly free associations and the ruled nature of disruptions of free-associating. Word-surprises are ruled disruptions. Nothing is irrelevant to the analysis, nothing need be wasted. (Wasting time is itself an action, as is making sure not to waste time.) That not everything gets to be understood or used during analysis is, of course, true, but beside the point.

To explain why the word-surprise occurs is to define the analysand's situation in such a way that the action of saying that word makes more sense than can be established in any other way. But since a change of situation is implied in the event—otherwise there would have been no word-surprise—one is further obliged to explain that change. And since situations are creative actions of developing some version of one's circumstances and courses of action, the analyst must ask why the analysand acted to change the situation. The analysand was not overtaken by the change; nor did the action happen to the analysand. Explanations of that type are inappropriately mechanistic. It is enough to answer this question to assert that momentarily the

surprising word had become the thing to say or no
longer the thing to refrain from saying, and to add that
this had come to be the case through whatever flux of
action and situation the analysand had introduced during the previous moments of the analytic session.

In brief, we are left with the answer that that is just
what the analysand did; what the analysand said was
what made the most sense to say just then. Making
sense is not limited to the speaker's conscious idea of
what would make sense or what is consciously intended.
In this respect the speaker clearly does not have the
last word on what it makes sense to say. My answer sets
up the word-surprise as a curious text, and it asks how
this text came to be written. This is to approach the
matter historically, not causally.

History and Causality

Thinking historically, we do not say an agent is causally motivated to perform some action by all the relevant factors in the historical background of that action.
We say that *this* agent did *that* and perhaps gave or
could have given *these* reasons for doing so, while another observer might suggest other reasons for it. But,
speaking of the historical factors that we consider relevant to the event, we do not designate them the *causes*
of the agent's action; we use them to define the action,
say, as a belated and displaced revenge on a younger
sibling.

In performing a certain action, the analysand might
or might not have been thinking of some life-historical
conflict consciously or even unconsciously, and yet the

analyst may legitimately claim that that conflict of long standing is an important feature of the action and its situation; it is an important feature in the sense that the action will remain unintelligible or less understandable if one does not suppose something of that sort. The interpretation says what the analyst must suppose to have been the current situation and the sense of the action, whether or not the agent has defined it as such. Factors A, B, and C in the analysand's life history must have figured in the coming about of the word-surprise; the surprising word is just what someone with that history and this correlated present situation would say, and that person would have changed the situation in just this way at just this point.

If we say that *this* action would be performed under *those* conditions, we are not using the term *conditions* in the causal sense. By conditions we mean that which it is necessary to take into account or to assume in order to understand the action in question. "How else could it be?" is what we want to be able to say. "No other descriptive account makes as much sense as this one."

To be more exact about psychoanalytic work, the analyst works backward from the word-surprise to arrive at some account of the situation in which saying the "wrong" word was the thing to do; and to reach that point the analyst must go back into the analysand's life history. In following this explanatory procedure, the analyst works within an interpretive circle: what is thought and how it is defined and arranged as life-historical background follows the same rules as those followed in defining the present situation. The history, the present situation, and the actions are correlative rather than logically independent. The context that is established is not a second context but a more complex context that covers a wider span of time than was initially thought to be relevant. When one interprets unconscious conflict, one is showing that the situations and actions are more complex and enduring than have seemed to be the case, and is showing particularly that they include paradoxical features. But never is one dealing with logically independent variables and so never is one engaged in developing a causal account. In saying why a word-surprise took place, one does not get to say which past events caused it. Instead, one works with a unified theory in which there is only one class of events, not two or many. All the events are on the same plane, though some are characterized by different features or modes. None has temporal or logical priority; all have explanatory utility.

This then is the logic, in the terms of action language, of the explanation of word-surprises. One no longer thinks, as Freud did in one aspect of his investigations, of a mental apparatus freed from constraints of reason and working on its own in a qualitatively different causal universe. This, for example, was the way he explained the coming about of jokes (1905b). To think this way is to legitimize disclaimed action in one's theory of free association and of mind, and it runs contrary to Freud's clinical mode of explanation. What the free associating does is make plainer the archaic rules that are being followed by the analysand. As one analysand said, "This room only seems to be a room without conventions." Just so, the analyst's attitude that there is no right or wrong in free association as such—an idea that analysands can hardly ever accept fully—points to the same principle of interpretation, namely, that judgments of right and wrong make sense only in the context of rules, that is, the conventions and categories each analysand uses to create the psychoanalytic situation, to set the meaning of free associating, and to go on to perform in that situation.

Thinking Coherently

One is working now with a scheme wherein the matter of thinking things in advance is merely one way of thinking, albeit an important one. Accordingly, one views each thought as originating in itself and not in a preexisting, causally compelling and organizing motive. The next question to face is this: Why is there any coherence at all in what we think? But one must question this way of putting the question: Why shouldn't we be coherent? In turning the question around, I am reversing one of Freud's fundamental assumptions; that our primary cognitive condition is incoherence. This is the assumption that, to begin with, thinking is completely under the domination of the primary process (1900), the pleasure principle (1911), the unconscious mode of mentation (1915), or the id (1923).

On this assumption, our primary mode of thinking is simply hallucinating the satisfaction of our needs, remaining oblivious of the limits and opportunities in reality, being insensitive to contradiction, failing to distinguish wish from fact or deed, and so on. This primary mode of thinking is in the service of immediately reducing the painfulness of instinctual drive tension.

Thus, from Freud's vantage point, the question would have to be this: How is it possible to think coherently at all? Establishing the dominance of the reality principle over the pleasure principle, or of the secondary process over the primary process, can only be viewed as a slow, arduous, and forever imperfect process; constant expenditure of mental energy must be required to maintain this dominance; and we are more than glad to regress—in sleep, play, or fantasy—to the archaic, essentially chaotic or incoherent condition. It is being presupposed that, to begin with, thinking follows no rules, that rules are imposed on thinking during development as a matter of coming to terms with reality.

Now, this point of view stands in marked contrast to the point of view that before anything can qualify as thinking, it must make sense in some situation or context and so must be a rule-following action. Or since it may be speaking that is in question, speaking makes sense only in some situation or other, and it, too, must be a rule-following action. To put the matter more generally, an action, in contrast to a reflex response or a bodily reaction to physical force, is a rule-following performance; otherwise it is no action at all, and so it is not a proper matter for interpretation.

On this view one can allow that, initially, the rules being followed by a very young child are simple, unrealistic, unobjective, unarticulated, and uncoordinated; one can further allow that mental development consists in the progressive revision, replacement, integration, and supplementation of the archaic rules with rules of a more reasonable, sophisticated, stable, and coordinated sort. In developing into a person, moreover, the child learns self-reflectively to be a rule-learner, a rule-follower, a rule-maker, and a rule-coordinator. But it cannot be the case that one ever functioned mentally without rules. Even Freud's (1900) paradigmatic case of hallucinatory oral wish fulfillment—according to him, the first instance of thinking—depends, as he noted, on a remembered experience of gratification. One must ask whether this dependence would not necessarily imply some primitive notion of coherence such that, one way or another, breast and gratification go together? Freud did not envision mental development as a reflex action or a conditioned response.

The only way around taking this action view of development is to take recourse to an essentially neurological reflex-scheme, such as the one Freud (1895) outlined in his now famous Project; it is a scheme he retained in psychological guise ever after (Gill, 1976). In this mechanistic scheme, prior experience establishes channels for the flow of excitation and facilitates that flow through lowered conductive resistances. Although this picture does perhaps capture some aspect of the neurological substrate of mental actions, it cannot represent actions as such. The picture of actions must be purely psychological and self-sufficient.

There is a stretch of time over which the very young child manifests its first actions. These are always performances that imply some directedness or aim; by the same token they imply some situation in which directedness or aim makes sense. We begin to view the child's activity as actions once we can say that they imply reasons, have meanings, or manifest intentions. They may be reflected upon and interpreted. Thereby we contrast them with mere reflex or physical responses to physical causes. Then we think or say the baby wants to be picked up, wants the rattle, is pleased to see us, is cross at us. Statements like these, when they are not overeager projections onto a neonate, imply that the baby is acting in a situation, is behaving intelligibly, and so is following rules of some kind. They may not be our rules, but they are rules nonetheless; consequently, they may be understood. We may, of course, be wrong about the rules the child is following; for instance, the baby may still fuss despite being picked up. And we may be wrong that the child is following a rule at all; for instance, we may be premature in our judgment. But mere possibility of error cannot vitiate the argument being advanced here.

That thinking or speaking is a rule-following performance is the basis of expecting to find coherence in free associations. It makes it legitimate, if not compelling, to ask why the associations shouldn't be coherent. So long as the analysand speaks consecutively, coherently, with appropriate transitional comments, with all the signs of being in some situation, the analyst may have little to say. Perhaps after a large dose of this kind of coherence, the analyst might mention that the analysand is presenting so seamless an appearance in the analysis that no analysis can take place, or in other words that this utter orderedness is a form of resisting analysis; the coherence itself must be a refusal, the taking of some kind of stand against the analysis. Utter orderliness does not correspond to spontaneous thinking and speaking; the analysand must be carefully preparing it and monitoring it.

But if the typical manner of free associating is less than orderly, does not that fact speak for Freud's view about, say, regression toward the unruled primary process? No. Even the metapsychologically oriented analysts do not believe this to be the case, for they assume that in principle every departure from perfect order is potentially intelligible; it is an interpretable utterance even if for the moment it is not yet understood. If it is intelligible and interpretable (which come to the same thing), it embodies the observance of some sort of rule or set of rules appropriate to some situation. It is just that the situation or context cannot be the one that so far has been taken for granted; at least, it cannot be simply that one. And this state of affairs is just what the word-surprise indicates. As we might say casually, "There is more going on than meets the eye"—though the analyst, aware of resistant actions, even then would have to add, "and more than the eye of the analysand is willing or prepared to see."

The Fantasy of Unruled Associating

In setting a plan, rehearsing a discourse in advance, picking a topic to talk about, the analysand is in one respect dealing anxiously with the imagined prospect that the free associations will be chaotic, which is to say that there will suddenly be no situation at all, no possibility of action or of being an agent, no rules to follow and so no personal history or personal continuity. This state of affairs or eventuality is viewed unconsciously, and sometimes it is likened consciously, to a state of craziness, helplessness, totally infantile regression, castration, incontinence, destructive explosion, or some other extreme possibility. In taking this view persistently an analysand will be indicating a state that he or she has chronically and characteristically desired and feared and with reference to which has conducted much of his or her life. This is to say that, subjectively, the free association situation is necessarily a danger situation, one that unconsciously stands for or amounts to the basic conflicts of the analysand's life. In agreeing to observe the fundamental rule, the analysand is agreeing to that which he or she desires and fears most. The analytic fundamental rule being viewed in this light, the analysand would make it a rule of his or her own to circumvent it whenever the going gets rough.

It is, however, a personal fantasy of loss of self or agency that is in question here, and not an empirical truth. Being crazy or incontinent or whatever does not mean the end of self or agency, as is feared; nor does it mean the end of continuity and conventions of any sort. For craziness, incontinence, and the like are also actions performed in the situations they imply. Unconsciously, the analysand recognizes this to be so. That is why one can analyze the fear of free associating on any such basis. The analyst knows that one cannot give up being human by consciously agreeing to follow or suspend any rule.

Thus, fearing to free-associate implies that the analysand expects to be acting in some other game with some other rules and dreads the consequences of doing so. There is, however, no exit from oneself, so to say, though there may be a change in position in the personal room one inhabits, and there may be more going on in that room and more options for rule-governed action than one has dared acknowledge to oneself, to one's analyst, or to both. In any case, those who are suitable for a psychoanalysis carried out on the basis of the fundamental rule are by definition so constituted as people that they never could come close to the condition of simply playing the most primitive games—the psychotic ones.

Conclusion

The general view we must take finally is that people act in far more complex ways and in far more complex situations than some forms of common sense would insist is the case; further, that some aspects of these actions and situations are marked by infantile, irrational, contradictory, imperiously wish-fulfilling features; and also, that the agent is most likely to be self-deceiving and opposed to enlightenment by others in connection with some or all of the seemingly chaotic and in any case threatening features of his or her actions. *The free-association rule makes apparent the nature and extent of this complexity.*

In this light it can readily be appreciated how wrong it is to say to someone, "I know what you are really saying"—or really thinking—or really wishing, for logically what is real should not come into question. That kind of statement is not even crude reductionism (that common accusation directed at analytic thinking); it is simply wrong. It would be right to say, "There are more ways than one of understanding what you are saying [or thinking, or wishing], and more than one way is required to make sense of it. You are doing more than you dare to realize." This way of putting it corresponds to a well-accepted principle of text analysis: there are more ways than one to understand a text; more than one view may be required; and the author's view of it counts as only one among others, and is a view whose authority cannot be taken for granted.

I want to put this point in its most general form. There are more ways than one to understand reality (Schafer, 1976). Reality is not, as Freud usually assumed, a definite thing to be arrived at or a fixed and known criterion of objectivity. Some ways of understanding reality are simply wrong, as in the case of saying that a person seems to be saying one thing and is "really" saying another. Other ways vary in their specific and general coherence and their explanatory power, and so some are superior to others. For example, some medieval explanations of natural or psychological events can be shown to be inferior to contemporary ones in their being more limited or less coherent. That the views of Rank, Adler, Jung, Reich, or Horney are inferior to Freud's can be shown in the same way.

The Third Lecture
SELF-CONTROL

The psychoanalyst works with an expanded notion of self-control. For one thing, the analyst ordinarily views control as only one aspect of the action under consideration; in its other aspects that same action may be unconsciously erotic, aggressive, or self-punitive. For instance, self-control may be tantalizing or frustrating to another person and masochistically gratifying to oneself. For another thing, one may unconsciously get others to control one's actions in some way that is desired, in what amounts to a form of projected self-regulation; children often behave this way. For a third, controlling oneself may also be a way of controlling real or imagined others, and this may be so consciously as well as unconsciously. One may, for instance, be unconsciously imagining a hostile internal figure whose influence must be controlled, or one may be unconsciously relocating one's own desires in another person and then controlling those desires through controlling that person.

The third instance comes under the heading of projective identification, whose influence on interpersonal relations can hardly be exaggerated. In projective identification, one controls one's own rage or depression or sexual excitement by controlling the emotionality of another person; in such cases that person will be being unconsciously viewed as the container of one's own emotional and wishful self. Projective identification becomes recognizable when the subject enacts those very emotions or desires, or reacts violently against them, once the control of the other person seems to fail. How often people get enraged, depressed, or manic when they cannot keep others about them happy, tranquil, forceful, or successful!

Viewing self-control from the opposite direction, it is often a matter of controlling that which one imagines one has incorporated from others; then one struggles with oneself as the container of the feelings and desires of others. This is introjective identification. The psychoanalyst often struggles with introjective identification before recognizing that he or she is enacting a certain kind of countertransference; experiencing as his of her own the analysand's envy or despair, for example. By dint of that realization, the analyst will be equipped to redefine the situation, reallocate emotions and desires, and establish grounds for an interpretation.

In everyday relationships, the participants ordinarily remain more or less oblivious of such unconsciously imagined interpenetration of selves. They view the issue of self-control narrowly and naïvely. Such is the case, for instance, when an adolescent son struggles, it seems, simply for sexual self-control in a situation where, in fact, he has projected his desire into his mother, has incorporated her desire into himself, and is acting subtly to excite her, just as she is concurrently doing to him.

The question of who or what is being controlled in self-control is one that must regularly be asked by the psychoanalyst in practice. Psychoanalytic studies of family members in interaction have amply confirmed the value of this approach. According to these studies, it is useful to view each member of the family as struggling to control a family problem that, unconsciously, is being experienced merely as one's own or as the problem of just one other member. This problem may be madness, dangerousness, inability to love, failure, or the like. Another case in point is Erik Erikson's (1956) discussions of negative identity: by negative identity, Erikson refers to a mission unconsciously assigned to a child *not* to become a certain kind of person, and this for the sake of his or her parents' defensive security and their conscious sense of personal and communal integration. The view that in self-control one is simply controlling one's impulses is an impoverished view of both human beings in relation and the ambiguities of self-definition.

Thus, according to the psychoanalytically expanded view of self-control, control is not just control but action and gratification as well, and self is not just self but others as well. Here is a clinical example. An analysand characteristically related each dream with many interruptions. Ostensibly these interruptions were necessary to allow the introduction of pertinent background on the figures, places, and events in the dream as well as to present already rehearsed associations. He performed this job so assiduously that finally the analyst was prevented from conceiving the dream clearly and freely formulating questions and conjectures of his own while listening; instead, the analyst experienced a growing sense of awkwardness in asking for associations to the details of a dream that had already been extensively worked over by the analysand. In performing these actions and creating these effects, the analysand was carefully controlling himself and making sure not to be surprised by anything he might think or say in connection with the dream; simultaneously, he was controlling the analyst, preventing him from having his own free analytic access to the dream. In the guise of analyzing

his dreams conscientiously, he was resisting the spirit of
dream analysis, for true dream analysis must be open to
the unexpected; otherwise there is no point in doing it.
Dream analysis is exploration of strange territory, even
if with sophisticated equipment; it is meant to turn up
something new.

This same analysand interlarded his methodical, ex-
haustive, and exhausting accounts with interpretations
of his own, doing so from early on in the telling. He
tried to limit himself to bringing up only what was
consistent with his interpretations. Although analysands do arrive at interpretations while they are free-
associating, they usually do so with some uncertainty,
surprise, or consternation; at least, it is spontaneous
interpretation of some such kind that may legitimately
carry some independent weight in the analysis. But to
produce interpretations of manifest dream elements
directly and systematically is not free association. It is
surprising, to say the least, how many published examples of dream analysis accept programmatic interpretation by analysands as sound analytic work.

In the case I mentioned the analyst had to interpret
not so much the dream and the associations as the meaning of how, in his reporting, the analysand was dealing
with both the dream and the analyst; and the analyst
had to do so in terms of interpenetrative controls. It
was this same analysand who, on another occasion,
dreamed of a fire set by an arsonist, an action with
respect to which he, the analysand, was apparently an
accidental bystander. Analysis of that dream concluded
with the analyst's interpretation that characteristically,
as well as in his immediate situation, the analysand

tried to inflame others with desire or anger while presenting himself either as a detached witness or as a passive victim of the others' excitement. Much evidence accumulated over the course of his analysis that this maneuver has originated in his relationship with a controlling mother and that he had continued to employ it in every one of his important relationships, including that with his analyst.

I have wanted to show, even if briefly and incompletely, the clinical complexity of interpreting self-control psychoanalytically, and to indicate how that job might get done. I shall have a little more to say about clinical interpretation, but in the main I shall be engaged in an extended critical examination of the idea of self-control. All of us learn, from early childhood on, to assign a central role to this idea; it is a role that shapes our ideas of ourselves as people and, consequently, our conception of human psychology. I shall emphasize particularly the way our adoption of the idea of self-control inclines us toward the dehumanizing language of mechanism. Inevitably, my discussion will clash with assumptions and practices that are dear to all of us, owing both to their place in our formative relationships and experiences and to their defensive value; and it may therefore generate some of the same discomfort and opposition on the reader's part as it has on mine while I've been trying to work it out.

Inadequate Self-control and Disclaimed Action

The idea of self-control may perhaps be best approached critically through taking up the questions of what it is to fail to exercise self-control and what it is to lose it. There are many familiar locutions for expressing failure to exercise self-control and losing control of oneself. We speak of giving in to an impulse or being overwhelmed by it; we say we couldn't control the impulse or that it ran away with us; we say that we couldn't control ourselves or didn't do so or wouldn't do so; we speak of getting back to ourselves or regaining possession of ourselves after losing control; and so on. Of each of these locutions the psychoanalyst may say that, unconsciously, it amounts to a disclaiming of action. Disclaiming takes the form, in effect, of making excuses in terms of inexorable and impersonal forces or sheer and unaccountable willfulness that is alien to the self. Action is being disclaimed in the sense that what has not been controlled is denied the attribute of intentional selfhood or agency. Even in the case of such locutions as "I couldn't control myself," which implicitly attribute selfhood to the actions in question, that selfhood is not the kind with which one is fully identified, and so is not the kind for which one consciously and definitely assumes the agent's responsibility.

Disclaiming of this sort implies a theory of mind or self that is not unified. The subjective idea of one's self is, of course, fragmented in these instances, but what I want to emphasize is that in each case the implicit theory of mind is itself fragmented. It is fragmented in that, in a self-contradictory way, it postulates two universes: one is a universe of more or less impersonal forces operating causally and the other is a universe of personal agents or intentional activity.

If one were to systematically apply the unified mechanistic theory of the first kind of universe, one would say something like this: The causes that determined the exercise of control were less powerful than the causes that determined the expression of that which remained uncontrolled. But that is not how we think of our conduct in everyday life; nor is it the essential way in which clinical psychoanalysts think when they interpret specific instances of alleged failure of self-control. In their clinical work they think instead of disavowed or disclaimed action (though perhaps they do so in other terms, such as acting out a fantasy or defensive failure). They think that the analysand has done something while also wishing not to do it and is now denying the true complexity of the action in question. In particular the analysand is repudiating the idea that he or she is as implicated in the allegedly uncontrolled deed as in wishing to exercise control. It is only in their extraclinical theoretical formulations that psychoanalysts attempt to give a thoroughgoing causal account of these actions, and they do so, not because their evidence warrants it, but because the traditional metapsychology requires every feature of a psychological event to be formulated mechanistically.

Having found, however, that the strictly mechanisticdeterministic propositions do not cover the ground adequately, metapsychologists have taken to speaking of autonomous ego functions (Hartmann, 1939). Autonomous ego functions are the adaptive functions that are said to operate with their own supply of noninstinctual energy or neutralized and uncommitted energy; that kind of energy is freely available to the ego for pursuing the objectives that it sets for itself. In speaking this way, metapsychologists would seem to have smuggled free will into their deterministic universe; however, it would be more correct to say that, far from dabbling in free will on an ad hoc basis, they are verging on the philosophy of free action as set forth, for example, by Melden (1961). In so doing, they are moving outside the realm in which the controversy over free will versus determinism has any point. In the new realm, the actions, even if irrational by conventional standards, may be redescribed and thereby explained in terms of their reasons; they are potentially intelligible actions of a more or less socialized person. In speaking of the ego's setting its own aims, the theoreticians of ego autonomy are referring to free actions rather than caused events. But they shudder at the thought that this might be so, as I once did, and they attempt to develop deterministic accounts of autonomy.

From a systematic point of view, matters are even more unsatisfactory than this, for one does not find the deterministic account of autonomous ego functions carried very far. Sooner or later it becomes evident that this is a job that cannot be done. One finds psychoanalysts taking recourse to the idea of *relative* autonomy, and with it to the idea of *partly* neutralized and *more or less* uncommitted ego energy, and these are ideas that reinstate the very problems the concept of autonomy was meant to solve. The idea of relative autonomy reestablishes the free-will-versus-determinism controversy. Relative autonomy is a futile gesture toward a thoroughgoing mechanistic-deterministic program, while unqualified autonomy destroys the possibility of a unified theory of that sort.

In contrast, the notion of disclaimed action that is being put forward here simultaneously defines manageable clinical problems and exposes concealed and unmanageable metapsychological problems. I plan to show that action language, unlike metapsychology, makes possible a unified psychoanalytic theory of mind or, more exactly, of action. Specifically, my plan is first of all to expose the ambiguities and paradoxes contained in the idea of self-control; in the course of doing that, I shall have some critical things to say about the way the term *self* (and, by implication, the term *identity*) has come to be used by many psychoanalytic theoreticians. Then I shall examine critically the uses to which concepts of motivation have been put in psychoanalytic theory; in this connection I shall question the logical coherence and the necessity of these concepts and their typical applications. Finally, I shall present an action view of conflict in which nominative references to drives, motives, and conflict itself play no part; however, the essential referents of conflict, which are so central to the general psychoanalytic enterprise as well as to the specific idea of self-control, will be preserved intact, if not seen more clearly.

The Referents of Self-control

All of us conduct a good deal of the business of living with the apparent help of the idea of self-control; particularly during certain phases of our lives. During adolescence we face pressing questions of controlling our sexual and rebellious tendencies, especially with reference to masturbation; typically we experience our masturbating as being both sexual and rebellious. We are busy with this idea of self-control much earlier, during the periods of toilet training, infantile masturbatory activity, and oedipal claims on our parents. At these times the incentive for self-control comes largely from actually or only imaginatively present supervising parental figures and their conditional love. Even earlier, though in a minimally defined form, we are busy with self-control in connection with delays in being fed and tended, being weaned, and observing the care of younger siblings or sick or wayward ones. Thus, in one way or another, self-control is a lifelong preoccupation.

But just what does *self-control* refer to? Does it refer to a self that controls, and if so what is the nature of that self? Does it refer to a self that is to be controlled, and if so what is its nature and how does it stand in relation to the exerciser of control; the other self perhaps? Alternatively, if it is not a self that is to be controlled but rather an impulse or desire, how is that mental entity or phenomenon related to what we call self?

Ordinary language suggests that self-control embraces all three referents: a controlling self, a controlled self, and something that is not self but is subject to personal control. It is immediately evident that to retain both the controlled self and the controlled not-self is to be logically incoherent. This is so because, within one system of explanation, something like an impulse either is a manifestation of self or is not; logically one can't have it both ways. But each of these referents presents logical difficulties, and to show this I must criticize these three propositions: first, and at greatest length, that the self controls the self; second, that the self controls the not-self; and third, that the controlling self is a necessary and useful theoretical concept.

Does the Self Control the Self?

To say that the self controls the self is to commit a category mistake in that controlling anything is one of the constitutive features, or one of the referents, of what we mean by self. We would not say that a thermostat controls a thermostat, for in one interpretation it controls a furnace of some kind or the flow of fuel into it and in another the temperature of a room or house. Similarly, we would not say that a government controls a government, for we would realize that government means controlling certain constituents operations and personnel. If the self exercises control at all, it must control something else. Consequently, when someone is admonished, "Control yourself," a logical mistake is being committed, even if the message seems to be understood (as many such messages are).

Let me say in passing that in examining the logic of our locutions we cannot be concerned with what seems to work for ordinary purposes. If we were to legislate in Draconian fashion in the realm of what works, we would be left with little that is familiar to say to one another or to ourselves when we are thinking. Why so many illogical statements nevertheless seem to be somehow effective communications is a significant question. My examination of the language of self-control should go some way toward answering that question; that is to say, it should clarify what meanings might be transmitted through intrinsically illogical and elliptical locutions.

It seems wrong, then, to speak of the self controlling the self. But before accepting this conclusion, we should consider two ways in which part or all of this idea might be salvaged. The first way can be dismissed readily. It is to attribute selfhood only to that which is being controlled, while giving some other name to the exerciser of control. It can be dismissed because few, if any, would assent to this solution, either in everyday life or in psychological theorizing. It would be right to reject this proposal. If selfhood is not to be attributed to the exerciser of control, the idea of self loses too much of its meaning. That selfhood may be denied to that which is to be controlled is, as I have said, another kind of solution, and I shall come to it soon.

The other way in which "Control yourself" might be salvaged as some kind of logically unobjectionable statement is to postulate that individuals have more than one self. This solution is represented in both ordinary language and psychoanalytic theory. In ordinary language one speaks, for example, of one's other selves, one's secret self, and one's better or worse self. One says, "Part of me wants to go and part wants to stay and I am torn between the two"; "I don't trust myself"; and so forth. In some versions of psychoanalytic theory one hears, for example, of the divided self or the authentic and inauthentic self (Laing, 1969), and the true and false self (Winnicott, 1958), and, when ego is substituted for self, of the libidinal ego and the anti-libidinal ego (Fairbairn, 1952).

Although this type of solution seems handy, it does

not stand up as a systematic solution. One of its difficulties lies in its dividing the person into a number of more or less independent agencies that operate according to different principles and so must be, in some fundamental sense, different sorts of entities. Indeed, it often sounds as if one person is in fact a group of radically different people, each acting autonomously and self-reflectively. Psychoanalysts know that people do think of themselves in this way, especially in their fantasizing and most of all unconsciously. For example, people imagine that they incorporate others, and they do not distinguish sufficiently what they simply imagine from what conventionally passes for reality. On this basis, people think they are inhabited by others, merged with them or living in their influential presence when, in ordinary fact, these others are not and could not be where they are thought to be. Psychoanalysts also appreciate that the claim of dissociated selves has considerable defensive or disclaiming value.

Now, this terribly important class of phenomena and strategies is what must be explained, and it is hardly an explanation to import the multiple-self fantasy into the theory and then use it to explain causally the multiple-self fantasy (cf. Thalberg, 1974). The theoretician who takes this task appears to be overawed by the content of fantasy; in effect, he or she is saying that that content is real in the same sense that the person who thinks it up is real. Many aspects of the psychoanalytic theory of internalization perpetuate this confounding of phenomena and their explanation. The result is that the problem has been shifted into the theory, where it can no longer be dealt with.

There are other difficulties with the multiple-self solution. How is one to decide how many selves there are? This question is like the one that used to plague the instinct theoreticians, that is, the question of how many instincts to postulate. In the course of Freud's development as a psychological theoretician, he essentially abandoned the late nineteenth-century goal of setting up a moderately large number of instincts—the so-called component instincts (sadistic, masochistic, voyeuristic, exhibitionistic, etc.)—along with the general sexual and self-preservative instincts. Advancing even further in his thinking, Freud shifted the emphasis away from instinctually dictated specific activity of any kind. Instead he finally emphasized two general classes of instinctual energy—the libidinal and the destructive—the specific aim and objects of which get established only in relation to the necessities and the accidents of maturation and development in a social world (Bibring, 1936).

A third difficulty is reification. I mentioned a number of dual-self theories that, structurally, are like Freud's dual-instinct theory: the authentic and inauthentic, the false and the true, and, although it is more complicated, the libidinal and the antilibidinal. These polarities set up two contrasting classes of phenomena with attributes of selfhood. In practice, however, they get to be used, not as classes of phenomena, but as causally efficacious and conflicting agencies. In this way they are reified. They are said to do this, that, or the other thing, when the justification for categorizing them at all is based on the observation that people do this, that, or the other thing, and on the further assumption that it will be useful to group these doings into two contrasting classes. Recognized for what they are, classes of phenomena don't do anything.

Another difficulty encountered by the dual-self theories is that most doings cannot be neatly dichotomized. In my opening remarks on the interpenetration of selves, I tried to show some ways in which this is so. It is only the overeager or overawed theoretician of the self who tries to make it seem otherwise. One may, of course, speak of authentic or inauthentic, or real or false, *aspects* of particular actions. And although some actions seem to be usefully or adequately described mainly in terms of one pole, that fact cannot justify the binary scheme. Just as personalities are neither simply introverted nor simply extroverted, and just as symptoms are neither simply instinctual nor simply defensive, actions are neither simply authentic nor simply inauthentic. It is always a question of our vantage point as observers, and the distance of this vantage point from the phenomena. To think otherwise oversimplifies matters. However, once one is working with multiple-self conceptualization, the alternative to dichotomizing is obviously a very troublesome one, namely, coining another self for every major type of action. This alternative is that troublesome because then one is free to create, on the one hand, a plethora of reified selves, and on the other hand, grounds for interminable and fruitless controversy, as in the case of the old multiple-instinct theories. In the light of these considerations one may well ask, "Why not stay

with the more or less complex and always redescribable
actions themselves, and dispense with potentially disastrous adventures in multiple-self psychology?"

Does the Self Control the Not-self?

The second of the three propositions I mentioned
earlier says that that which is to be controlled should be
designated not-self. The advocate of the not-self view
must immediately face the question of how else to designate it. It has already been mentioned that this view entails disclaiming of action in its denying the attribute of
selfhood to the repudiated. I have also pointed to the
desirability of establishing a unified theory.

The very fact that a psychological theory requires
two or more qualitatively different entities, processes,
or phenomena renders it suspect from the first. This is
so because each such type of entity, process, or phenomenon implies a distinct and exclusive universe of
rules and terms suitable for propositions concerning it.
A theory in which self coexists with nominatively designated drives, impulses, or desires is suspect for this
reason. One must ask, for instance: What can self have
to do with an impulse? For self, unless it just means
the person, is somehow or other an experiential phenomenon, a set of more or less stable and emotionally
felt ways of telling oneself about one's being and one's
continuity through change. In contrast, an impulse,
drive, or desire is an entity in some hypothetical physics
of the mind, an impersonal force characterized by direction, quantity, velocity, or acceleration. In its nominative designation, an impulse, drive, or desire cannot

be the action of a human being, that is, a performance whose description refers to or implies personal meaning, goal-directedness, reasons, and responsibility. It is necessarily an entity that stands behind personal action or, as we often say, underlies it.

Just how could one ever get from mental physics to mental phenomena? To say that the former gives rise to the latter is no answer to this question, for there are no transformation rules to get us from one to the other. We cannot conceive of their continuity. Nor, for the same reason, is it an answer to say that the mental becomes necessary owing to the disastrous effects on the infant of primitive, automatic mechanism operating alone, which is to say that the shocks of reality enforce the coming into being of the mental. This account presupposes what it is intended to explain, namely, learning about the world, a phenomenon of mind. And to say that maturation makes cognition possible, and thereby experience or mental phenomena as well, does not get us very far, for even though this statement offers little to quarrel with, it does not answer the question under consideration.

Consequently, it seems desirable to approach this question differently. In ordinary thinking, one inevitably takes account of bodily organs, needs, and reflexes, however primitively one does so. On the basis of ordinary language-learning, one comes to designate some events *processes,* other events *controls,* and still others *self* or *controlling self.* But in any *theoretical* endeavor that one would claim to be unitary, one's propositions about cognition would refer only to cognitive processes and contents; they would not refer to factors of some other sort. In everyday life, we may be used to thinking about mental forces, but in unitary theorizing we cannot say that a thought deals with a force. A thought does not deal with anything, for it is not an agent. It is the thinker of the thought who is the agent. It is the thinker who deals with things. The self is a thought, not an agent. The self is a kind of telling about one's individuality. It is something one learns to conceptualize in one's capacity as agent; it is not a doer of actions. In this light, we can see that Heinz Kohut (1971) and other analytic theoreticians of the self have been wrong in speaking of the experiential self as playing its own regulatory role in human action.

Taken as a manifestation of human action, the self may be changed. Often it is changed by the further action of changing one's selective and self-reflective discriminations, interests, and goals, as one does in the course of undergoing analysis. In this sense, the self is a regulated mental action, a telling rather than a teller.

Is the Idea of a Controlling Self Needed?

I have left behind the discredited notions of the controlled self and the controlled not-self, and have been criticizing the proposition concerning the self that says that the self as controlling agent is a necessary and useful theoretical idea. That proposition might now be defended, in the light of the preceding discussion, by saying that *self* just means *person*. It is, of course, permissible to use the term *self* to refer to the person as agent, that is, to use *person* and *self* synonymously. However, the term *self* is not usually used this way.

Instead it does double duty: it refers to an experiential entity that a person constructs, and at the same time refers to a regulatory agency that defines experience and prescribes activity, that is, the self-system as a rule-making and content-assigning organization. This equivocal and self-contradictory use of the word *self* cannot answer the question of what we could mean by a controlling self. Only an adequately unified theory can be satisfactory. As I mentioned in discussing the metapsychological approach, its aim is to develop a unified theory of mechanism. For instance, it sets up the mechanistic ego to control mechanistic drives or impulses, as by the use of defenses. But this aim has never been satisfactorily achieved. Indeed, the present hypertrophy of self concepts *within* traditional metapsychology is a reflection of the inadequacies of the attempt at a unitary metapsychological scheme.

Although to use *self* and *person* synonymously is permissible, it is desirable to use only one term in systematic propositions. This term should be the one that is the more direct and unequivocal, the one that is closer to the idea of agency in its established sense. That term is *person*. Not *self*, not *identity*, not *ego*, but *person*. Self and identity are representational actions of a person; ego, divested of its mechanistic trappings, is a class of actions and modes of action or aspects of these, that a person performs.

It would be wrong to think that what is being objected to is the reduction and organization of data that are necessary parts of any scientific enterprise. The objection is to the received idea of psychoanalytic science. What is being proposed is another idea of what it is to develop systematic psychoanalytic propositions. I am proposing, that is, a different kind of psychological world, and so a different way of understanding psychoanalytic data and of reducing and organizing them. Whatever psychoanalytic work has shown to be important remains much the same in this new world. One continues to speak of people, for example, as doing things unconsciously as well as consciously; establishing transferences and resisting analysis; loving and hating themselves and others; and doing some actions predominantly in the ego mode rather than the id mode or in the superego mode rather more than in the ego mode, and so on. In time one might even drop the terms *id, ego,* and *superego* and still use classes of actions and modes that do the work of these terms, and do it more exactly and coherently. The names are not sacred. I shall return to these structural concepts in the next lecture on self-love and self-hatred.

Both the self that does the controlling and the self or not-self that is controlled now stand revealed as actions by which we tell, in more or less organized fashion, what we do. That is to say, we present our actions and modes of action in the past, present, and future, under certain self-referential descriptions. Taken in any other sense, these self-concepts involve us in many logical difficulties.

The problem that remains before us is how to translate such statements as "I lost control of myself" and "My self-control was equal to the occasion" into logical statements. This will require a reexamination, in the context of action language, of the concepts of motivation and conflict. But first some further consideration of the concept of self is in order, because of the importance we attribute to it in all of our accounts of subjective experience. That importance serves as a major implicit support of the more specialized concept of self-control.

The Corporealization of the Self

Through infantile fantasizing and its perpetuation in ordinary language, the self is commonly taken to be some kind of place and substance. We are all familiar with this corporealization of the self. We speak of the inner self and of reaching into oneself, perhaps deep down; we think of the self as being invaded or shattered, empty or emptied, opened or closed off. In its materiality, the self is that which occupies some space, and in ordinary language we even find the self paradoxically represented as the surround as well as that which is surrounded. A statement such as "I retreated into myself" presents the self in both aspects.

It may be objected that these are matters that can only be rendered metaphorically. Would you deprive us of our metaphors? What will become of the richness of subjective experience? These questions—or should I say demands?—lead into problems of language that require extensive discussion in their own right in order to do justice to their fundamental importance for any theory of thinking and the construction of experience. For the present I must limit myself to a brief discussion of two points.

The obvious rejoinder is that the intent and character of logical examination of language is not legislative with respect to ordinary or clinical usage. In saying what we do do, I am not saying what we must do or must stop doing in our nontheoretical discourse. To say that the idea of self-control has illogical features is not to say that it must no longer be used in interpersonal transactions or informal thinking. Even though I am also using examples from everyday speech or thinking to develop my argument, I am aiming my criticisms at those aspects of systematic language or theoretical propositions that are imbued with these features of ordinary language.

Second, I must attack the logic of challenge itself. The claim is, with respect to metaphorical rendition of some experience, that there are no other words for it. "For what?" I would ask. If there are no other words for it, that is, if there is no other expressible referent, then the "it" is the metaphor itself. To say that there are no other words for it is to seem to claim that there is a known something else that corresponds to the "it"; but if that is so, then there must be other nonfigurative or minimally figurative words for it. In this connection the proper claim would take some such form as: "This metaphor is as much as I think of saying in this connection, and I am satisfied to say only this much." This way of putting it is consistent with the idea that the metaphor *constitutes* the experience and is not *about* an experience understood as some other known event. Thus, when a metaphor is labeled an approximation or a pale version of the real thing, or in some similar way, it is being implied that more would have to be said before one would judge the statement to be satisfactory: perhaps the metaphor is not as rich in allusions as one would like. The speaker could make no other claim than this.

It must be allowed, of course, that the coiner or user of the metaphor may be able to explain or defend its aptness and, in doing so, may say something about the "it" that the metaphor was intended to express. But, except in the case of deliberate introduction of metaphor for rhetorical purposes, when one has the "it" and wants merely to dress it up, this exegesis of the metaphor would be its decomposition and so would transform the experience; it would not be a way of getting back to some pure, independently existing, utterly nonfigurative prior experience.

Returning now to the spatial and material metaphors of the self, they should be regarded as ways of creating or constituting the self rather than as descriptions of an entity already fully known in other terms. The self-metaphor is self-experience proper rather than some version of the experience of a self-entity. Metaphor may *imply* other experience; in that respect, although it may say something about other experience, it cannot be simply equivalent to something else. To put the point in its most general form: experience, far from ever being preconceptual, must be conceptualized along some line or other and in some context or other in order to qualify as experience. There can be no raw experience in the sense of language-free and contextless phenomena, no experience that one conceptualizes only after observing it introspectively. Metaphor is one way of creating experience. A "shattered self" or an "empty self" is a metaphorical creation of experience by a person. It takes a person to say of himself or herself "I am empty" or "I am torn between the two parts of myself."

Were one to shift, for example, from saying "shattered self" to saying "as if I were shattered glass" or "I imagine myself to be some kind of substance shattered," one would be transforming one's experience, even if only slightly; one would not be giving an altered account of some knowable and fixed phenomenon.

In *A New Language for Psychoanalysis* (1976), I have attempted to show that much of the psychoanalytic theory of internalization has been based implicitly on the uncritically used metaphor of self (or mind) as place and substance. Here, again, there has been a confounding of phenomena and their explanation. It is the very importance of these phenomena that calls for the strictest consideration of theoretical approaches to them.

Motivation and Self-control

From this point on I shall dispense with self concepts as such and take up the concepts of motivation and conflict. These two concepts, being primary constituents of the psychological language of everyday life and psychoanalysis, are centrally implied by the idea of self-control, which rests on them. Self-control obviously implies *conflict*—for the idea of self-control to make any sense, that which is to be controlled and that which controls must be viewed as standing in opposition to one another. And, according to familiar usage, self-control equally obviously implies *motivation*— where self-control is in question, one motive must be opposed to another, or one set of motives opposed to another set; moral motives opposed to sexual motives, for instance, or defensive motives opposed to aggressive motives.

It seems that self-control must be a matter of conflicting motives. Conflicting motives seem to be the psychological referents of any psychology that is called, as psychoanalysis is called, dynamic. In this connection, the special contribution of psychoanalytic work to psychology as well as to the individual analysand seems to be its study of unconscious motives, so-called: psychoanalysts study their aims and their infantile, bodily, sexual, and aggressive origins, and they study the motives of repression and other defenses that keep the infantile motives unconscious and so perpetuate their archaic influence on adult life.

I have been saying what *seems* to be the case because one may legitimately question whether it is necessary to adopt the language of motivation and build it into the idea of conflict. This question arises as soon as one realizes that the use of motivation concepts is a sophisticated way of explaining human action; it is not an observed and simple fact of nature (whatever that is, if it is anything at all). Admittedly, it is difficult to realize that the use of motivation terms represents a conceptual choice; these terms so pervade contemporary language that they may be called constituent elements of our learning to think in any way whatsoever about ourselves and others as human beings.

Every one of us has been brought up to believe without question that, in some form or other, human action can only be accounted for by invoking motivation

terms. I am referring to motivation terms of a particular
sort, namely, those that say that there is something that
makes one do whatever one does This is a something
that impels, propels, compels, drives, enforces, or demands that one do something. This presupposition
goes far back in time, at least as far back as the time of
visitations by the gods directly or through the natural
elements and creatures that are divine instruments
and manifestations. We just believe that we would not
do anything unless something made us do it. We accept a principle of human inertia and a view of human
beings as instruments of other agencies. In one of its
aspects, this presupposition rationalizes disclaimed action, in that it sets the motive or desire apart from the
person, establishes it as the true agency of the deed,
and reduces the person to being merely its vehicle or
executive apparatus. One may enjoy considerable com-
fort, security, or pleasure through consciously believing
oneself to be that passive and free from responsibility. We should not underestimate these pleasures,
grounded as they are in the young child's formative
relationships with parental figures. But, in our theoretical endeavours, much is lost by carrying this view
of things over into our notions of what unmistakably
exists in "nature."

My claim is that this kind of motivational presupposition gets in the way of our arriving at the best designations of the actions we hope to explain. It does so,
first of all, by suggesting that it is perfectly clear what
these actions are, that nothing more and nothing different need be said about them. It bypasses the poly-
thematic nature of actions and the contextual basis of

interpreting action. It suggests that the real explanatory task lies in saying what prompted the taken-for-
granted actions. And it suggests, moreover, that the
designation of what prompted an action is logically
independent of the action's designation and its context
or situation.

But the designation of the action is neither self-
evident nor context-free; nor is the designation of the
motive logically independent of the description of the
action viewed in context. Supplying a propulsive motive for an action may be condemned as a split-up, cum-
bersome, and mechanistic way of arriving at another or
a modified contextual description of the action. Every
action has at least one intentional description. As mentioned earlier, naming the intention plays the part of
giving the reason or sense of the action; it does not play
the part of stating its causal force. It is true that in
some explanatory schemes, *motive* is used for the purpose of giving an intentional description: but why not,
then, just say *reasons,* if that is what one wants to say;
or why not just designate the action without referring
explicitly to its reasons or intention, if that is all that
is wanted or is most appropriate? For example, "Anxiety is the motive of defense" may be restated, "People
undertake defensive measures when they view their
situation anxiously, that is, as a danger situation";
"Your desire for success made you reckless" may be
restated, "You sought success recklessly"; "Your sexual
drive overwhelmed you" may be restated, "You engaged in sexual actions no matter what—indiscrimi-
nately"; and "Libidinal motives are determinants of
all human relationships" may be restated, "People act

erotically (or lovingly, tenderly, etc.) in all of their relationships."

It is systematically possible—even if, for the time
being, it is perhaps personally disagreeable—to speak
of all these things without taking recourse to driving
or causally efficacious motivations. To speak so would
be to use action language consistently. There is no
need to postulate one class of unconscious causes and
another class of conscious reasons or intentions, as
some have proposed. Nor is there logical coherence in
the idea that through psychoanalysis a greater range of
autonomous action is made possible; for to use that
idea is to presuppose that there are two distinct classes
of events, namely causal unconscious happenings and
rationalizable free actions. The considerations I am
advancing apply equally to actions performed in situations that have been defined unconsciously or consciously.

Motivation as the moving or causal force is necessarily prior to that which it causes. In following the rules
of action language, one may not invoke any prior moving force as a justification for considering something
an action and as a means of arriving at its best designation for the occasion. Let us return at this point to the
action of free-associating, and let us consider it now in
its aspect of decreasing the exercise of "self-control" in
the realm of thinking, speaking, and feeling. It follows
from the preceding remarks that one is barred from
saying that free-associating is initiated, shaped, extended, blocked, and organized by unconscious motives
operating as forces, determinants, or causes. It is permissible and advantageous simply to say this: When

one follows the fundamental rule of free association, one thinks and says things that imply in some
of their aspects—not all—certain consciously repudiated themes that characterize certain contexts of action and situation. Typically, in what is called *resistance* or *defense,* the analysand repudiates these implications more or less anxiously and decisively as soon
as it is suggested that that is what he or she is doing in
one or another context. This stressful time may come
only after the analyst makes an interpretation, though
it may come spontaneously when one is surprised by
one's own words or feelings.

Nothing in the analytic work is altered by the adoption of this revised view of the nature of free associating and psychoanalytic interpretation. The psychoanalyst continues to define the psychoanalytically familiar
conflictual themes and to trace the same sorts of infantile origins of these themes, though perhaps he or
she does so more lucidly now owing to a clearer conception of what it is possible to say coherently. The important task of the psychoanalyst is to decide on those
psychoanalytic descriptions of problematic actions and
situations that are the most illuminating and potentially
the most conducive to beneficial personal transformation.

Conflict and Self-control

I have been trying to show that the use of action
language enables us to dispense not only with self
terms but with motivation terms as well. I have entered
into these considerations in order to clear away con-

fusing presuppositions about the idea of conflict and its appearance in the idea of self-control. What now can we refer to coherently as the constituent elements of conflict? This question also asks what we can mean by the term *conflict* itself. Speaking from the vantage point of action language, I have been suggesting that it makes no systematic sense to speak of conflicting parts of the self, of self conflicting with not-self, or of motives conflicting with other motives.

This is what I propose instead: (1) limiting our propositions to actions and modes of action; (2) in the case of conflict, speaking of actions or modes of action that are incompatible with one another or stand in paradoxical relation to one another; (3) recognizing that somehow or other these paradoxical actions are being simultaneously performed by one agent, if only in the realm of wishing; (4) including as one of the actions involved in conflict the agent's realizing, unconsciously or consciously, that the actions and modes in question are paradoxical while more or less refusing to refrain totally from performing any one of them; (5) having granted that wishing or desiring is one type of action, installing paradoxical wishing or desiring as the ultimate referent of conflict; and (6) no longer referring to conflict as a logically distinct and causally efficacious phenomenon, but speaking instead of a person's acting in a conflicted manner or conflictually. In this way one may discard or elude the dehumanizing mechanistic conception of conflicted human existence and go on interpretively to redescribe the relevant phenomena in the terms of a unified theory of action.

To take an example from everyday life: on a particular evening one may wish to go to the theater and simultaneously wish to stay home and read a book, and one will be acting conflictually to the extent that one keeps on wishing to do both. Or to take a familiar example from psychoanalytic work: unconsciously, one may wish to engage in incestuous relations with one parent and simultaneously wish to avoid the dreadful consequences this action would have on one's relations with the other parent or both parents, and one will be acting conflictually to the extent that one goes on wishing to do both. Similarly, one may, unconsciously, go on wishing for a sibling's death while condemning oneself for doing so; or one may wish to be loved, admired, and protected by one's analyst while also wishing to abuse and destroy this same figure. In each such instance, people will indicate, sooner or later and directly or indirectly, that they are acting conflictually by what they do publicly, by what they think or imagine wishfully, and by the emotional modes, especially the anxious and guilty modes, in which they behave in these situations; they will indicate it also by performing apparently disrupted actions, such as making slips, concentrating poorly, developing symptoms, and doing all the other things that have long been recognized as conflictual in everyday life and defined more richly and subtly through psychoanalytic study.

In this view of acting conflictually, there is no place for pseudoquantitative statements about the relative strength of the different constituents of conflict. This is so because each constituent refers to a person performing various actions, in which respect it makes no sense to say, for example, that a man is weaker than himself or a woman stronger than herself. The apparently quantitative aspect would now be dealt with by a suitably complex redescription of the correlative actions and situations. One of the things to be described is how urgently the person performs any of the constituent actions in question; we have many qualitative criteria of what it is to do something urgently—or feebly, casually, etc.

Resolution of conflict would be dealt with in the same way. That is to say, such resolution would be viewed as the person's redefining the paradoxical actions and their situations in such a way that they are: (1) no longer paradoxical, (2) no longer the only possibilities envisaged, (3) no longer the principal issues, (4) no longer the actions to persist in, or (5) some combination of these. It may, for example, no longer seem paradoxical to a woman to be both a woman *and* intellectual or to be psychologically both masculine *and* feminine according to usual criteria. Similarly, a young man may get to envisage other possibilities than being either a slave or a tyrant, in which case the issues of power will no longer be paramount in his considerations. Or one may finally learn to accept—as it is necessary to do—that, inevitably, one includes paradoxical elements in one's major, complex actions, and that this feature is not necessarily best described as a failure of synthesis.

What Do We Mean by Self-control?

To exercise self-control is to follow a course of action in a consciously conflictual manner, that is, while wishing instead to follow another course of action that one condemns. In following this favored course of action, one defers engaging in the repudiated actions, altogether refrains from doing them, or attempts to give up wishing to do them by such means as setting up blocks to their performance or transforming them into less extreme, less incompatible, and more acceptable actions. It is always the *person* who defers, refrains, or transforms, and it is always a *course of action* that is being repudiated or modified; never is it some other self or animated force.

To fail to exercise self-control or to lose it is to perform the condemned actions. One acts while telling oneself not to act or not to act in that way and while deploring the fact that one nevertheless acts so.

Both exercising and failing to exercise self-control thus refer to those instances when one acts conflictually and constructs a dramatized representation of this mode of action. References to specific reasons for resorting to these representations will be found throughout these lectures; generally speaking, these reasons, which apply to all fantasy activity, have wish-fulfilling, defensive, self-punitive, and adaptive features. In this dramatization or fantasy of self-control, one takes two parts: a cautious, prudent, or tyrannical self and a wild, impetuous, unruly self. There are a hero and a villain, a good child and a bad child. Alternatively, the second or controlled self may be portrayed more or less explicitly as a creaturelike or machinelike set of impulses, forces, or mechanisms. The different versions of this fantasy are so embedded in our everyday language that they have been accepted as a "natural" model of conflict, to the detriment of theoretical clarity and consistency.

To say *why* the person does or does not perform the condemned actions is to establish another designation of them: on the one hand are such designations as playing it safe, being tactful or compromising, remaining consistent, taking no further interest in alternatives, or misrepresenting what one would do under other, safer circumstances; on the other hand, there is acting recklessly or immoderately along sexual, aggressive, self-destructive, or egoistic lines. Explanation in terms of action of the vicissitudes of self-control thus dispenses with assumptions about the existence and temporal priority of substantive, autonomously active wishes, desires, or motives, and other such factors which allegedly cause, impel, and organize action. In these explanations, one does not refer to people acting *on* or *because of* wishes, desires, or motives; nor does one refer to people acting *against* or *in spite of* pressing forces or insistent other selves. Every aspect of intentionality is referred to one and the same person and is expressed through the use of verbs and adverbs. The intentionality in inherent in the designated conflictual performance; it is not its precursor, external ruler, or vanquished foe.

Also to be emphasized is the elimination of the idea of achievement from the actions referred to by "self-control." These actions are not matters of "can" or "can't." Self-control is a way of acting, however dramatized the subjective narrative of this way of acting may be. Even the term *self* is dispensed with in the strictly formulated action account, for that account speaks only of a person performing a complex action in a distressed and ambivalent manner. Thus, instead of saying, "Her self-control was adequate to the occasion," one might say, "She consistently refrained from doing some of the actions she wished to perform in that situation." And instead of saying, "He lost control of himself," one might say, "Although consciously he wished not to act intemperately, he did so anyway." In both instances, one may fill in the details of action and modes of action with as much detail and vividness as necessary. In this way it remains clear that one is describing actions. And one of the actions it may be clinically important to describe—for theoretical purposes it is essential to describe it—is the action of constructing a fantasy in which there is a cast of characters involved in self-control. The subjective representation of the embattled self should not be imported into, and confused with, its systematic description of a person acting conflictually.

The Fourth Lecture
SELF-HATRED AND SELF-LOVE

In psychoanalytic work one often hears people confessing such feelings as "I loathe myself," "I am a worm," "I hate myself," "I don't deserve to live," and then further confessing that they have been doing things to hurt, punish, or even destroy themselves. The psychoanalyst also hears people proclaiming, sometimes enthusiastically and sometimes ashamedly or anxiously, "I'm better than everyone else," "I'm terribly proud of myself," "I'm delighted with myself," "I much prefer my own company," and other such feelings, and then further acknowledging that they have been giving themselves pats on the back, presents, body kisses or mirror kisses, and loving caresses. Although self-loving and self-hating actions are not restricted to the psychoanalytic session, they soon stand out there, and they come in for much attention during the analysis. More important perhaps than their obvious forms are their subtle, implicit forms—the shrug or flat tone of voice that is somehow self-annihilating and the silent loftiness or veiled gleam in the eye that walls off the beloved subjective self from the surrounding world.

In the course of investigating these self-hating and self-loving actions, the analyst finds them to be riddled with irrational beliefs and practices. It is found, for instance, that people hate themselves for misfortunes that have befallen them during their childhood; they blame themselves without warrant for having been neglected, for parental unhappiness and death, and for severe illnesses. This is excessive claiming of action and is the opposite extreme of the excessive disclaiming that was mentioned in the preceding lectures. To give another example, it is also found that people love

themselves maternally as a way of substituting a sem-
blance of the primary bond between mother and infant
for present-day relationships with others; often they
act in this way for defensive reasons, that is, in order
to refute their own severe self-criticisms and feelings of
having been abandoned.

With respect to examples of these kinds, analysts
speak of disorders or instabilities of self-love, self-
esteem, or narcissism and of the harsh superego or
grandiose ego ideal. They stress the role of guilt, shame,
and defense in self-hatred and self-love alike. They distinguish between the omnipotent, self-defeating forms
of self-love and the moderated, socialized, and constructive forms, such as those they see developing during the
course of an effective psychoanalysis. They also distinguish between the destructive and constructive roles of
self-criticism and self-imposed prohibition. Especially
in recent years the topics of self-love and narcissism
have been in the forefront of psychoanalytic concern
(see, e.g., Kohut, 1971; Kernberg, 1975). Earlier, the
varieties of self-hatred and guilt had been emphasized.
Even though many analysts have shifted the focus of
their technical and theoretical explorations in this way,
they continue to regard guilt and self-hatred as crucial
factors in both personal development and therapeutic
need and responsiveness.

It is, therefore, warranted to subject the ideas of self-
love and self-hatred to close logical scrutiny. This is
the kind of scrutiny they seldom get in the psychoanalytic literature. There, it is usually taken for granted
that everyone knows what is meant by *love, hate,* and
other emotions and what is meant by *self* and *other as*

the sources or objects of those emotions. Analysts tend to write and talk as if there are few or no problems of knowing in these respects. It is as if all that is needed is a dynamic account of causes and historical origins. It was with this same warrant that, in my previous lectures, I worked over the ideas of life history, free association, and self-control, and, in the next, shall re-examine the concepts of impotence and frigidity. Specifically, I want to try to get clear on what we can sensibly mean by *self-love* and *self-hatred;* that is to say, I want to define the legitimate kinds of knowledge-claims we can make with respect to these basic, powerfully felt features of the way human beings experience and judge their own lives. Note that I am centering, not on the abstractions *libido, aggression,* and *psychic structure* with which Freud (1923) was increasingly occupied in his theorizing, but on the more concretely descriptive actions of loving and hating with which he had been much concerned in the earlier phases of his creative work.

I shall devote the first and by far the longest part of this lecture to an analysis of the idea of self-hatred. In this connection I shall indicate the approach to the concepts of emotion and emotional quality and quantity that seems appropriate for an action language. Aggression in particular will then appear in a new light. Next I shall take up some problematic aspects of Freud's theory of the superego as a regulatory and punishing psychic structure, particularly questioning whether the continuity or regularity of self-hating actions requires or justifies Freud's structural theory of the psychic apparatus. In the concluding part I shall

apply the results of the preceding discussions, appropriate changes being made, to the analysis of the idea of
self-love.

If carried through completely, the conceptual analysis of self-love and self-hatred would not run parallel
in every respect; however, these analyses do encounter
many conceptual problems of the same sort, and it is
only these problems and not every feature of self-love
and self-hatred with which we shall be concerned.

Self-hatred

Because, when we speak of self-hatred, we take the
person as both the subject and object of hating, it may
be expected that the analysis of the term will be facilitated by first taking up the case of one person's hating
another, moving then through the subject's being hated
by someone else and the subject's hating someone else,
and arriving finally at one's hating oneself.

One person's hating another   How do we use the word
hating when we speak of one person's hating another?
We use it to say that the hater regards the other as an
extremely dangerous enemy of some sort and attacks or
wishes to attack the other physically or mentally, as by
hitting, biting, soiling, torturing, annihilating, utterly
scorning or reviling, or totally suspending support, interest, or tolerance. Some of these actions are, so to
speak, hot and others cold, and they range from physical violence to silence. Thus, hating takes in a family
of actions and modes of action, some of which, descriptively, have little in common with others. Conse-

quently, some people rarely, if ever, hate in all the ways that others do, and standardization of word usage must remain far from strict. And yet ordinarily we know, and agree with one another, when one person hates another.

But how do we know? On what basis do we agree? We do not rely on the hater's words alone, for we know that words, whether in the form of expression or of testimony, can mislead us. What we do in fact is establish a case for the hating. This is so even though, in what we call intuition, we often make our judgment consciously before we have formulated that case. In such instances we assume an obligation: at some point we could develop the case for our judgment consciously and communicate it, or should be able to, for an intuition that is not at least a forecast of some kind of confirmatory evidence is of no practical use. On these grounds, if we tell one man that he hates another man, he in turn can sensibly ask, "How do you know that I hate him?" and demand that we present our case. If our case is faulty, he can then present convincing evidence against it; if it remains altogether undeveloped, it will in time carry no rational weight.

What kinds of evidence would be in question in this dispute as to what is the case? One kind is made up of the actions that are included by convention or rule within the family of hating actions. A second kind is what is excluded from that family as being incompatible with it. And the third kind includes the many actions that seem relevant but remain ambiguous.

Although it is not always easy in practice to settle a dispute of this kind through an appeal to evidence, it does make sense to try settling it, and people do try. One basis of the difficulty is a fact with which psycho-analysts are especially familiar; it is that this is a realm in which either-or decisions are the exception rather than the rule. This is so because some measure of am-bivalence toward the other person is likely to be felt by anyone whose believings, doings, and wishings-to-do seem to justify the use of so strong a word at *hating*. In other words, as a rule one has to care a great deal in order to hate; otherwise one might just be intermit-tently annoyed, indifferent, or dismissive. Another source of difficulty lies in the fact that ordinarily peo-ple distribute or displace the constituents of their am-bivalences defensively. On this basis, for example, if the alleged hater cites as evidence against hating his acts of benevolence and tenderness toward the other person, one could respond, perhaps wrongly but still sensibly, with the following interpretation: "This is your way, consciously or unconsciously, of disguis-ing your hating, disguising it possibly even against your own recognition. Not that this action necessarily amounts to pretending; it is just that, while your acts of benevolence and tenderness are genuine enough, you overemphasize them in order to disclaim your simultaneously hating that person; in other words, in order to deny your ambivalence."

The exchange I just described is not necessarily a naturalistic account of clinical dialogue, but it does set forth schematically the logic of a common psychoana-lytic interpretation. For example, this logic may be fol-lowed when an interpretation is made of the analy-sand's unconsciously ambivalent relations with parents, children, or spouse. In making this type of interpretation, the analyst will be relying on evidence distilled from dreams, fantasies, errors, choice of words, tones of voice, expressive movements, etc.; the analyst will be relying as well on contradictory public actions, such as professing love and yet being hurtfully indifferent to the loved one's feelings or interests.

Adjudication of such disputes soon encounters considerable complexity, owing especially to the coexistence and defensive alignments of opposites in mental life. Nevertheless, the rules of evidence ordinarily followed in making a judgment, or in explaining it after the fact, remain the same.

But now another set of complications is likely to arise from disputes as to the rules themselves. For example, in his defense, the alleged hater might say of a certain piece or collection of evidence, "I wouldn't call *that* hating! I'm just standing up for my rights emphatically!" Here the problem is one of descriptions that follow competing rules, the result being that one description confirms hating while the other refutes it. Yet adjudication remains possible and sensible here, too; at least it does so in many cases, for one may investigate and define further the context of the actions in question and the content that is implied in their form. If it is just a matter of standing up for one's rights emphatically, one is not likely to make slips of the tongue, such as, "If you're right, I'll eat my hate"; nor is one likely to dream of the destruction of the other person or too readily lose one's temper with him. Thus, in making our judgments we would still be working with flexible conventions or rules for naming and sub-

suming actions, and we would be marshaling evidence
for judgments about the emotions accordingly. And
these conventions or rules would specify actions and
modes of action, where action would be understood to
include initially private mental acts such as believing,
wishing, dreaming, and unconsciously overemphasiz-
ing. In this approach, the emotions—for example, hating—appear as sets of practices described according to
their context. They do not appear as autonomous mental processes, affective precursors or by-products of action, or happenings.

The subject's being hated by another person   Turning
next to our judging that we are being hated by someone
else, it is evident that in this endeavor we are guided
by much the same kind of considerations as those referred to earlier. We know and allege that we are being
hated by what the other person does or seems to wish to
do and by how that person does it or would wish to do it.
If, through report or surmising, one gains access to the
other person's dreaming, fantasizing, and other initially
private actions and states of bodily feeling, as one does
as an analyst, one has even more to go on to make the
case. Still, we may judge wrongly, or, when we are
making either-or judgments, we may judge one-sidedly
and so half-wrongly. If either error has been committed, the other person may be able to show that we
are judging the case wrongly or one-sidedly. Our intuition may be keener in those instances that concern us
directly than in those that concern other people, but,
as before, we cannot forever waive the obligation to
present or at least describe the regulated evidence
promised by the intuition.

What is distinctive in this connection, however, is that we may begin our case for being hated by noting that we are "feeling" threatened, defensive, worthless, empty, or abandoned; for it is on the basis of such feelings that we might correctly infer that we have been experiencing the other person's hating us without our having realized it. In this way, that is, through analysis of countertransferences, the psychoanalyst often correctly infers that he or she is being hated by the analysand; ideally, however, the analyst communicates this inference only with the support of other observations and interpretations, such as the interpretation of form as content and the implications of the analysand's free associations, dreams, and other analytic data. Even so, in this endeavor, the analyst is merely in a better position than the lay person to know about this subjective experience and its implications, and is not using rules of knowing that are qualitatively different from those followed in common sense. It is not rare for people in everyday life to make the same sort of interpretation, even if more globally. To tell someone, "You rub me the wrong way," implies this interpretation.

The subject's hating another person Consider next the case of our hating someone else. Here we do seem to encounter genuine qualitative differences in what we know or how we know it. This seems to be so because, as haters, we may claim to know without mediation that we feel just that way toward the other person; we tend to think that it would be absurd to be asked, "How do you know you feel that way?" Our own hating seems as immediately knowable as a pain or an itch. But suppose we are asked the better question, "'Why

do you say *hate?"* or "Why do you call that *hate?"* We
may, if we are not absolutely raging, give the questioner
more of a chance. We might reply, for example, "It's
hate all right! I want to kill that so-and-so! I hate the
very sight of him and wish I never had to see him again!
I'd love to get my hands around his throat [here making
squeezing gestures and raising our voices]. He can drop
dead for all I care!" Although these elaborations may,
from one important point of view, be regarded as sheer
expressions or performative utterances, in that they
qualify as *enactments of* hating rather than *talking
about* hating, they may, from another point of view, be
taken as answers to the question of what we mean by
hating. That is to say, we mean by hating certain things
we do or wish to do, including what we say or wish to
say to the other person or against him; we also mean
what we wish would happen to him.

Once again we are following the same rules or engaging in the same practices of knowing. We cannot stand
by our claim that we experience emotion without mediation, nor can we justify our repudiation of the idea of
the hating's being a matter of strategies of naming and
arriving at judgments. Whatever qualitative differences
in knowing there may be in the case of our hating of
others, they recede in practical importance.

It may be that all we can rightly insist on is that we
just thought or said *hate* unreflectively; no longer can
we sensibly reject the call for regulated evidence, even
if it is to be assembled only after the fact. It is, after all,
not so rare that we tell ourselves at some later time, "I
thought I hated him but see now that it was more
complicated than that"; or we may acknowledge, "I

hated him without knowing it." These are changes that we can only make in conformance with rules, using the evidence these rules require or imply. That is why we say, "I see now" and "without knowing it."

In their clinical work, psychoanalysts frequently encounter passionate declarations of hatred that, functionally, are last-ditch defensive measures undertaken against recognizing loving or sexual developments in the transference, or frightened or guilty developments in it. These phenomena are, of course, familiar enough in literature and drama, as they are in our own worldly experience and independent reflexive activity. When it comes to the emotions, the world recognizes that seeing and knowing are easily compromised and often revised; it does not take unmediated and unmistakable emotion for granted.

Quantities of hatred It will strengthen the foundation of my argument to call into question two preconceptions about hating in particular and the emotions in general. The first is that there are directly quantifiable aspects of hating. According to this preconception, hating someone more or less intensely may be taken to mean expressing or experiencing the charge of a quantity of emotional or motivational energy that is characterized teleologically by its aggressiveness. This quantitative way of taking emotion is a commonplace of everyday life, and it was used by Freud (1920) as a basis for postulating the primary instinctual energy of the death instinct (though he made his way to this postulation along a number of other routes as well). To many people, psychic quantity in some materialistic or

quasi-materialistic sense seems to be an inevitable assumption, if not an immediate experience. It has the
aura of rooting human beings in lawful nature.

I shall not argue that it is impossible or absurd to
develop useful scales for making comparative estimates
in the realm of the emotions. Such scales exist and have
been useful in psychological research. I do, however,
want to point out several necessary features and consequences of these scales. First, they must be based on
descriptions of emotional actions that center on their
frequency, duration, directness, focus, scope, and consequence of any physical movement and physiological
arousal that may be involved. All such accounts refer,
not to quantities, but to heterogeneous descriptive features based on interpretation. They are quite unlike
homogeneous readings of quantity on a linear physical
gauge. Second, these scales must depend as well on
additional interpretive conventions concerning what
should count as a greater quantity of emotion, such as
hatred, than something else. Third, these scales lead to
conclusions that are false for individual cases even
though useful for mass experiments or correlational
studies, for no such scale can adequately represent the
importance of taking context into account when describing or interpreting actions. Finally, in quantifying,
one is likely to bypass the phenomenological richness
of the emotion that is being studied.

The psychoanalytic method stands in contrast to the
use of rating scales. Within this method, one makes
judgments based on comparative phenomenological
considerations which are intertwined with life-historical
knowledge, especially as these are presented in the

psychoanalytic situation, and most of all in the analysand's transferences and acts of resistance. Even then, these judgments are not altogether unambiguous, and often they have to be revised subsequently, at least through being made more complex. To put these abstract holistic remarks concretely in the form of a question: What, for example, would be our warrant for saying that hitting someone else frequently is more angry or hateful than thinking consciously of hitting someone else for the first time, when, in the first case, we are speaking of a habitual exhibitionistic brawler and, in the second, of a man who has always acted in an extremely inhibited and repressed fashion? Also to be taken into account is the fact that for some people apparent acts of hating are sadistic, which is to say that they are sexual in their unconscious significance, and that in this respect they do not qualify as mere acts of hating and possibly do not qualify as hating at all. And what of a cold, still hatred that, far from being characterized by volatile presence, is evidenced by devastating absence? Finally, in the case of a hateful action, might we not be witnessing an alteration of defensive strategy rather than increases or decreases of quantifiable aggression?

Accordingly, one may more safely, and a bit more simply, compare each person with himself or herself, and one must allow for its taking an entire analysis to establish the hateful significance of a particular action, say, a disabling symptom or a sexual limitation. In the light of these considerations, the notion of a native, directly apprehended quantity of energy faces away into deliberations about holistic redescriptions of actions and the relativistic methods of establishing and connecting the so-called facts of the case.

In the lecture on self-control I touched upon an important and relevant theoretical problem: that the quantitative conception of emotion is connected to the assumption that specific actions require propulsive forces behind them in order to occur at all. I tried there to show that this assumption, which spawns the concept of psychic energy, is neither necessary nor unassailable.

Unlearned hatred   Another important preconception about hating and other emotions must be called into question. According to this preconception, hating is an unlearned or natural description of how we feel and so, as a description, is incorrigible. But the fact is that *hate, hating, hatred,* and the like are words we learn like any others. We learn how to use them with reference to a certain family of situations, actions, and modes of action. As with the words *love, good,* and *bad,* we may be taught them poorly, we may learn them poorly, and we may use them wrongly, that is, ignorantly, defensively, too absolutely, or at least carelessly. And, as with all other words, we are potentially accountable for our word usage within one or more language-games. For instance, if a man declares that he hates someone else, he may be referring merely to being annoyed but, owing to his having learned a dramatized set of rules for describing situations or actions, he may not make the distinction that would be made according to ordinary language rules and that would therefore be anticipated by the ordinary listener. However, it will not do to say on this account that each person's hating is just what he or she says it is. We can be corrected in what we say about our emotions, and, as I noted, we may and often do correct ourselves sooner or later. In making such corrections, we use some standard language-game as our criterion, even though optimally the rules of this game must remain flexible, if not loose. They had better be flexible in the case of such consequential emotion words as *love, hate, good,* and *bad.* The flexibility being an aspect of the rule, it, too, is learned.

Thus, the emotion may be viewed as a matter of usage. It is knowable through socially acquired and modifiable practices. None of which denies that fantasies and bodily concomitants and activities are among the constituents of what, finally, we call an emotion, such as hatred.

One's hating oneself   Thus far it has been argued that, fundamentally, the same problems of knowing exist whether we are speaking of one person's hating another, one's being hated by another, and one's hating someone else. Additionally, it has been argued that it is naïve to deal in ideas about directly accessible quantities of "hating" energy and unlearned and incorrigible knowledge of what hating is. Now at last we may turn to the question of how to think of self-hatred, that is, one's hating oneself. Are matters here any different, and if so, how?

The idea of self-hatred is reflexive in its characterizing the person as both subject and object. What must be added is that the idea of self-hatred may be doubly reflexive, for one may also tell oneself about this self-hatred. This possibility complicates matters, but not hopelessly. I shall not belabor the point that we may hate ourselves without consciously telling ourselves that that is what we are doing. In daily life, and all the more in the psychoanalytic situation, one is able to say to people who are blind to the fact, perhaps insistently or defensively blind to it, that they do hate themselves. Nor need it be argued, at least not in the light of psychoanalytic investigation, that in specific instances one may be as inaccurate in claiming to hate oneself as in claiming to hate others. The claim will be inaccurate, for instance, if it is incomplete, inexact, or histrionically enlarged. That is to say, the self-hating may be, respectively, also a defensive obscuring of overweening pride; a masochistic, that is, sexualized form of self-flagellation; or an exaggeration that is part of an established strategy of self-dramatizing. In the first instance, one does not simply or mainly hate oneself; in the second, one is practicing an obscure, though not rare, form of sexual activity; and in the third one is making a move in an asocial language-game that, upon close inspection, shows little plausibility and is being played desperately.

In all these instances of hating oneself, the types of evidence and the principles of interpretation are much the same as those involved in the instances of hating discussed earlier in this lecture. That is to say, one deals with the same expressive movements, language usage, dreams, fantasies, bodily states, and patternings of actions of every kind. And the person continues to be established as the hater in the same way as before and also as the one being hated. But now the hater and the hated are one and the same person—the persecutor

is also the victim! Also, under this action-oriented description, the emotion involved is not a separately discoverable, autonomous entity; nor is it specially privi-
leged or ultimately inaccessible to others. Rather, the
self-hating refers to a set of practices, that is, actions and
modes of action, of which the action of telling oneself
or others that one hates oneself counts as only one item,
and not a decisive one at that. It is the enactment of self-
hating that will be decisive. In this connection, Freud
(1923) emphasized the enacted need for punishment.

I want to develop the point that in self-hatred the
persecutor and victim are one and the same person.
This is obviously true in one sense, that is, in common
sense or the sense of ordinary consciously defined experience. In the psychoanalytic sense, however, it is
true only to a limited extent. Psychoanalysts are particularly concerned with what is unconsciously wished,
believed, imagined, and perpetrated. Unconsciously,
the persecutor or the victim in self-hatred may be someone other than oneself, or part of that other person, or
any fluid or fixed merging of one's ideas of self and
other. For example, unconsciously, the hater in self-
hatred may prove, upon analysis, to be an idea one
holds of one's father; through fantasied incorporation
or identification, this paternal figure has been unconsciously installed in the subjective self as a hating
agency. It may, however, be only the paternal phallus
that has been thus installed. Alternatively, the subjectively internalized father or paternal phallus may be
the hated object rather than the hating subject. It may
even be the case, unconsciously, that both the persecutor and the victim are other persons, say, one's father in

the act of hating one's mother; here, "I hate myself"
translates into "In this way I enact, experience, and
perpetuate my father's hating my mother."

In this connection, we are encountering once again
the interpenetration of selves that was discussed in the
lecture on self-control. The hated self proves on analysis to be a cast of characters that includes especially
fathers, mothers, siblings, and former selves, or any of
their symbolically significant organs or characteristics.
These figures are, of course, selective, distorted, and
fragmentary versions of these people and their parts
rather than faithful representations of them; they are
idealized, derogated, split-apart, and confused versions
of others—imagoes, so-called.

Nevertheless, it will remain a case of self-hatred,
whatever these constituents may prove to be. This is
so because these imagoes are necessarily one's own
ideas, however much they may be based on actual
people and events (Schafer, 1968). It is the subject who
is now imaginatively playing the parts of these others:
one hates oneself in their name, or one hates them in
one's own name, or one just keeps them hating one
another in one's own medium and name. For example,
it is not the incorporated mother imago who hates us
for our damaging greediness; it is we who are portray-
ing her inflicting her reactive hatred on us, and who
perpetuate that portrayal, often for defensive reasons.

The point that it is all one's own ideas is so obvious
that it should go without saying. Unfortunately, however, the psychoanalytic literature teems with statements that refer simply to the introjected mother's
hatred and portray the analysand's part as having to

cope with this figure as with some autonomous agency, as though having been possessed by a demon playing out its own nature. Analysands do often define their experience as being possessed and present it that way to their analysts; these accounts of subjective experience must, of course, be taken quite seriously. Nevertheless, possession by introjects cannot figure in any final rational interpretation of the experiences in question. When analysts empathically recognize archaic and dramatic versions of experience, they do not thereby arrive at any rational interpretation of it; nor do they yet have the concepts necessary for a good theory of interpretation. To believe otherwise is to establish a psychoanalytic demonology. The experience, viewed as a construction, must be interpreted.

Although self-hatred is interpreted in much the same way as the other cases of hatred, this phenomenon does seem to be descriptively different in certain respects. It cannot be otherwise, for in the other cases one of the parties is objectively a more or less independent or uncontrolled figure, while in self-hatred everything is one's own doing in the autarchic world of imagination and action on oneself. Not every hating action that one person may direct against another can be exactly duplicated in self-hatred, and some hating actions may be performed only in self-hatred. But I shall not enlarge on these points here.

A summary statement   To conclude this part of the analysis of hating oneself, I shall redescribe it in the most general way as more or less chronically regarding oneself angrily. This generalized redescription recognizes, first, that hatred is a complex version of anger, and that the two words cannot always be clearly distinguished. Second, it recognizes that the hatred with which one is likely to be especially concerned in analysis refers to acting angrily in some relatively abiding or fixed manner as distinct from limited momentary raging; and third, that self-hatred presupposes self-regarding or reflexive activity. The advantage of this redescription of self-hatred is twofold: it brings the discussion close to the psychoanalytic theory of the superego, that observing mental structure which regulates self-directed aggression; and, through being stated in terms of verbs and adverbs, it is consistent with the rules of action language.

The Superego in Self-hatred

I have already presented some of the advantages of shifting our conceptualizations away from nominatively designated parts of the personality, such as the self, and away from nominatively designated emotions. Instead of trying to characterize these hypothetical entities, I have recommended using verbs and adverbs to characterize the actions of single agents: instead of a divided self, a person acting in paradoxical fashion; instead of hate empowering aggressive actions, a person acting hatefully. But I have not yet addressed the topic of Freud's final tripartite structural theory of the mental apparatus, that is, his theory of the id, ego, and superego as regulatory psychological structures that act independently and carry on relations with one another. One of the main warrants for postulating the existence of these three structures is the high degree of consistency with which people perform their primitively wishful actions (the id), their defensive and adaptive actions (the ego), and their moral, self-hating and self-punishing actions (the superego). It is, however, necessary to question whether the idea of psychic structure explains these consistencies.

Because the superego structure is centrally implicated in the psychoanalytic explanation of both self-hatred and the impediments to self-love, I shall take the superego structure as the test case in the context of this lecture. First I shall synopsize Freud's account of this structure. Then I shall give an abbreviated account of the theoretical job Freud was trying to do in setting up this structure within his metapsychological theory, with special reference to the explanation of consistency or continuity of action. I shall argue that Freud's account is unsatisfactory and that a nonstructural account in terms of action and mode of action is adequate to the job. With this much done, I shall turn to the topic of self-love.

In the main, Freud (1923) attributed consistency of self-hatred in the neuroses to the superego. According to him, it is the superego which exercises that archaic moral self-criticism that is experienced as unintelligible guilt rather than normal pangs of conscience or self-criticism; and it is the superego which enforces that stringent self-limitation and drastic self-punishment that can shrivel up and destroy a life. The superego never altogether forgives the infantile "sins" of greed, destructiveness, and ruthlessly incestuous desire, and it judges harshly any symbolic expression of this "sinfulness" which may be attempted in later life. In effect, the superego hates us for having been the children we once were and have in part remained.

This agency is erected on the model of the prohibiting and punitive parents, especially the father, as magnified and distorted by the intensely emotional and magical infantile mode of understanding. It rules according to the talion law.

The superego works mostly unconsciously, and the energy with which it is empowered and which it expends in its operations is the instinctual energy of the death instinct that has come to be called aggression. Although the superego serves other functions, its fundamental psychoeconomic function, according to Freud, is to harness the otherwise self-destructive energy of the death instinct and to put that energy in the service, archaically construed, of renunciation, retribution, and socialization. In Freud's view, the superego is a lasting authority within the mental apparatus, never to be basically altered, always the channel of aggressive energy turned on the self, and defined by its functions of enforcing standards and punishments. On this account it warrants being designated a psychic structure. Here, the concept of psychic structure is used as it is in the case of ego structure: ego structure is defined by its stable and more or less organized defensive and adaptive functions and by its independent allocations of energies derived in the main from libido.

But, one may ask, what was Freud trying to account for or achieve by this structural superego theory? A full answer would require a review of the history of Freud's theorizing up to his writing *The Ego and the Id* in

1923. A few main features of his attempt may be mentioned without, I think, distorting the history of psychoanalysis. From the standpoint of his developmental psychology, Freud was trying to establish a force of sufficient magnitude to oppose the powerful incestuous wishes that make up the child's Oedipus complex. From the metapsychological standpoint, however, Freud was attempting a further defense of the hypothetical psychic energy, libido. Libido had been a mainstay of his general theory of sexuality and the ego for a long time. On the basis of various clinical observations and theoretical considerations, he had already concluded that libido could not account for all aspects of self-hatred; interpretations of the sexualized sadistic or masochistic aspects of this hatred could not do the whole job. And yet, he reasoned, some empowering energy had to be behind this phenomenon, as behind all phenomena.

For this reason among others, Freud (1920) had already introduced the idea of the death instinct with its destructive energy. But his having done so had given rise to a problem of systematizing: having already sketched the evolution and useful disposition of libido into the structure and functions of the mature personality, henceforth to be called the ego, what was now needed was a structure and a set of functions of comparable kind and stature that would account for the evolution and useful disposition of aggression. This new structure would make the psychoanalytic theory of instinctual vicissitudes balanced and comprehensive. The new structural theory would enable one to give a more systematic account of the ego, and in its superego aspects, it would account for intractable guilt, negative therapeutic reactions, and apparently senseless, repetitively self-destructive or painful patterns of behavior. And the theory would at the same time give an account of everything in energic terms. But as soon as one discards mechanistic and teleological notions of qualitatively different psychic energies, and, even more so, as soon as one is working in the context of action language, this monumental theoretical enterprise appears wrongly conceived.

There is, however, a third and less remarked feature of Freud's superego theory that must be criticized here. That feature is his preconception that continuity of attitude or feeling cannot be explained without reference to an enduring structure or organization that underlies this continuity and guarantees it. Freud had reasoned in the same way with regard to the structure, ego.

It can be shown that this line of reasoning is inevitable in any systematic developmental account of the personality that takes as its starting point a mechanistic picture of the newborn infant as the repository of imperious and mercurial instinctual energies; for these energies would have to be harnessed and regulated by enduring, automatically operating structures in order for development of any kind to take place and for adaptive activity of any sort to be guaranteed. And one of the marks of development and adaptive activity is the stability or continuity of what one does. For Freud, just as there could be no action without underlying quasi-physical propulsion, there could be no continuity without underlying quasi-physical structure. Propulsion and structure of this sort are the legitimate children of the wedding Freud had arranged of psychoanalysis to a mechanistic natural science. I am suggesting, of course, that this was not a fortunate match, or at least that it has not remained a happy one.

The question whether we need the idea of structure to account for consistency must be understood and answered differently as soon as one begins using non-mechanistic action concepts in an effort to develop an alternative account of what psychoanalysis is about; that is to say, an altogether different account is called for as soon as one abandons the idea of instinctual energies that initially are utterly mobile and that remain essential features of the personality.

A psychological account of consistency in terms of action need specify no more than that there is consistency *under certain descriptions* of the actions in question. In psychology, this consistency is often redescribed as a trait or disposition, where these terms merely refer to the regular appearance of a certain property or action; they say nothing about underlying motivations, energies, impulsions, channels, or regulatory psychological structures. This account of actions does not imply that a trait or disposition is an entity that somehow is always "there" in the person and is subject to complex psychological descriptions. A trait or disposition, being just a specialized description of consistency of action, is nowhere at all.

Furthermore, even if it made sense to speak of "thereness," one would still be in difficulty. This is so because the consistency in question exists only in connection with rules of redescription, the consequence being that any psychological structure is there only in so far as the observer is applying certain rules of description to a variety of manifestly varied actions. For instance, to say that someone is consistently careless will require re-description of actions of all kinds in such a way as to highlight their careless aspects; these actions will include tardiness, slovenliness, inattention to obligations and restrictions, etc. There may well be some lasting neurophysiological modification of the organism that is the concomitant of this consistency of action, but there is no psychological content we may attribute to that modification. The psychological content is the content of actions and modes of action as described by an interpreting observer with a certain interest and according to certain rules that implement this interest.

For example, Freud would say of a man who felt guilty about his successes and undermined them by contriving in all sorts of ways to have "hard luck" that he seemed to have a severe superego; this superego would be said to regularly punish the ego for unconsciously enjoying, say, oedipal triumph through worldly success. Speaking in a less obviously anthropomorphic vein, one might say that the superego, through its prohibiting, criticizing, and punitive functions, continuously exerted a hostile "influence" on the ego for being too much in the service of the wishful instinctual id or not sufficiently repressive in relation to the wishes of the id. This mode of explanation rests on the preconception that nothing would be explained by saying that, for reasons which in principle may be ascertained, the man consistently reacts guiltily to his successes and, in keeping with this mode of reacting, undermines them; it supposes that explanation begins by positing a structuralized autonomous agency in the mental apparatus that accounts for the consistency of this kind of action. But this is only to move the problem of explanation one step further away from the phenomena in question.

The problem here is the same one Gilbert Ryle (1949) took up in his discussion of what it is to know a tune. He argued that knowing a tune is not equivalent to playing it continuously "in one's head"; rather, knowing that tune is demonstrated by a family of actions such as humming it correctly, noticing mistakes in its performance, recognizing different renditions of it, etc. In the same way, the superego refers to a family of self-judging and self-undermining actions that are performed consistently in certain subjectively defined situations. It is an archaic moral way of acting, both emotionally and behaviorally. That consistency is established by interpretation of manifestly varied actions so as to bring out the archaic moral aspects they have in common. Redescription is necessary in order to define the successes in a way that is coordinated with forbidden gratification and self-punishment; nothing of relevance is always simply presented as such, either in dreams, transferences, or everyday life. The explanation of this consistency or continuity lies, not in positing a special psychological agency that is like a second self, but in giving a history of this kind of consistent self-punishing that is coordinated with an account of what one is punishing oneself for.

Thus, a conceptually clarified explanation that still followed the classical clinical line would refer to the man's punishing himself for unconsciously enjoying oedipal triumphs, punishing himself on the model of a

prohibitive and punitive father imago with which he
has unconsciously identified, and unconsciously equat-
ing his self-imposed failures with well-deserved castration. More of an explanation might be needed, but its
extension would be of the same kind. It would not be
of the radically different kind that requires a quantity
of death instinct embodied in a psychic structure that
combines all the features of a second self—all in one, a
policeman, harsh judge, and executioner.

Psychoanalysis has nothing to say about the biological modifications of the organism that may be the concomitants of these consistencies. It is a unique set of
interpretive practices that observe their own rules of
evidence, support their own claims to knowledge, and
are conveyed in their own language. No quasi-physical
structure is needed for regularly hating oneself in certain situations or in connection with certain actions,
including wishful imaginings. We are adequately
equipped with empirically established rules for using
the terms of archaic moral principles in our psychoanalytic redescriptions. These rules define classes of
actions and specify implicit continuities or regularities
where, manifestly, there may be only a jumble of
frustration, suffering, "hard luck," "sinning," and self-
reproach.

This critique of structural concepts shows that the
concept of structure, as proposed by Freud, describes or
names consistencies of action; it does not explain them.
These consistencies remain basic reference points for
psychoanalytic interpretation. Seen in this light, they
are close to modern nonmechanistic structuralist
theory.

Self-love

Rather than traverse the same route as that taken in the analysis of self-hatred, I shall simply summarize the main points of the entire foregoing argument by transposing them to the analysis of the idea of self-love. This combined summary and transposition will conclude this lecture.

We use the word *loving* in fundamentally one and the same way when we speak of one person's loving another, one's being loved by someone else, one's loving someone else, and one's loving oneself. That is to say, in each case we follow the same interpretive practices and language rules for including some actions and modes of action within the family of loving practices. The family is large and varied, and the rules of redescription are flexible; consequently, it may be said of different people that they love themselves even though each does so in a more or less individual manner.

In the case of loving we do not rely only or primarily on what people verbally describe or express about themselves and others; nor do we rest content indefinitely with intuitions that never forecast confirming evidence. "How do you know?" or "How are you using the word?" are sensible questions, to be answered by descriptions or redescriptions of actions.

As with hating actions, we include under loving actions all the initially private mental acts that we call dreaming, wishfully fantasizing, believing, and the like. As a rule we find ambivalent loving rather than pure loving, especially when we investigate its exaggerated

or arbitrary instances. Although adjudication of contradictory claims about individual instances of loving is
difficult, in principle it is neither absurd nor impossible.

Loving, like hating, should not be regarded as symbolically unmediated or unlearned; nor is it to be considered the expression or discharge of a measurable
emotional or motivational energy, termed *libido*. Such
formal or informal scales of self-loving as may be constructed will necessarily be based on tallying qualitatively or phenomenologically different kinds of observations; each such tally may be given weight only according to one or another convention of interpretation. It
cannot be applied in the holistic clinical psychoanalytic
situation, and it cannot be treated as a simple reading
of quantity on a gauge. It is bound to lead to error in
individual cases.

In self-love, the self that loves and the self that is
loved may, unconsciously, correspond to ideas one has
about others, about oneself, or about both. Thus self-
love involves the same varied cast of characters as self-
control and self-hatred. The characters are, however,
the puppets of one's own imaginings; for theoretical
purposes, they cannot be said to lead demonlike or
angel-like lives of their own. We don't encounter them;
we think them and we tell ourselves that we encounter
them.

The important instances of self-love of the sort that
correspond to those of self-hatred, as previously discussed, may be redesignated "more or less chronically
regarding oneself lovingly." The entire designation
being based on action language, the self or person will
be understood to refer to an agent characterized in one

way or another by his or her actions and modes of action.

The traditional metapsychological term for this realm of self-loving action is narcissism. Narcissism has been considered to be the investment of libido in self-representations rather than in representations of others. This libido is said to emanate from the id and ego structures. Metapsychologically speaking, libido may be more or less desexualized, sublimated, or neutralized; its teleological nature may be attenuated. Consequently, the phenomena of self-love range from sexual perversions involving grandiose fantasies, through vanity and egotism, to sheer enjoyment of one's doings and normal pride based on realistic standards and objective appraisal of the extent to which one approximates them.

But narcissism need not be taken to imply a continuous state based on an energy that is supplied, harnessed, and distributed by enduring psychic structures that act as other selves. That is to say, the metapsychological account need not be accepted. In action terms, narcissism is a set of regularly performed self-loving practices; it is consistently acting in certain self-loving ways in certain subjectively defined situations. Further, it is a pattern of action that is defined by using that regulated method of contextual redescription which warrants being called psychoanalytic. Through their special mode of redescription, analysts find self-hatred being enacted in myriad manifest forms. In the same way they find self-love being enacted endlessly—sometimes adaptively, sometimes defensively, and often self-destructively, that is, in the fashion of Narcissus of the myth.

The Fifth Lecture
IMPOTENCE, FRIGIDITY, AND SEXISM

Impotence and frigidity, whether actual, imagined, or anticipated, are two of the most pervasive and abiding concerns of men and women. And there is hardly another human concern that is so imbued with irrational thinking. As a rule, impotence and frigidity are taken to be failures of the worst kind. Esteem for oneself and others rides precariously on sexual performance and one's idea of what this performance signifies. Some who live in the shadow of these concerns desperately avoid sexual intercourse and even social relations, while many others desperately keep proving to themselves or to the world that they are not impotent or frigid or that they have no reason to fear being so. These concerns with impotence and frigidity also disrupt relations with friends of the same sex, owing to the shame, bravado, competitiveness, and plain dishonesty to which they ordinarily give rise. Moreover, through what is customarily called *displacement,* men and women manifest these sexual concerns in areas of life, such as physical, occupational, intellectual, and social fitness and worthiness. Although these areas seem far afield from sexuality, unconsciously they are more or less invested with sexual significance. In the end, there may remain few aspects of life that are not haunted, unconsciously if not consciously, by these concerns.

It is to be expected, therefore, that psychoanalysts will have learned a great deal about direct and displaced expressions of these actual, fantasied, and anticipated disturbances. Simply describing the phenomena in question and summarizing what has been learned about them would be justified if one did no more than that. Indeed, that description and summary would require a series of lectures, not only because there is so much to describe and so much that has been learned, but also because psychoanalysts differ among themselves as to what it is most important to describe and explain and how to do so. But I want to do a different job than that, and so, in these respects, I shall have to be relatively brief, schematic, dogmatic, and incomplete. I shall devote only the first part of this lecture to some well-established descriptive and explanatory highlights, and I shall set these forth in the terms of Freudian psychoanalysis. This much will set the stage for my particular undertaking. Although much of what I have to say will be familiar, it will serve as an explicit statement of what I take to be true.

This undertaking has two parts, each of which depends on the other for its full realization and so cannot be discussed separately. One part of the job is to show how impotence and frigidity may be viewed as actions and described and explained in the terms of action theory and action language; the other is to show how issues of sexism may be discerned in the typical ways observers define and appraise the phenomena in question. That is to say, in addition to sexism in the relations between the sexes, there is sexism in the very conception of these relations. The interdependence of these two discussions—of sexual actions and sexist conceptions—resides in discriminatory ascriptions of personal agency; that is to say, the traditional sexist ideas of what it is to be a man and a woman, or of the relations between the masculine and the feminine, bias one's observations of sexual actions from the first.

The best way to do this job is to center my discussion on Freud's notion of psychical or psychological impotence and, though he did not speak of it as such, psychical or psychological frigidity. For it is through the explication of these notions that one can appreciate the usefulness of the key terms of action language, namely, *person, action, mode of action,* and *situation.* Taking this approach, I shall be better able to clarify how psychoanalysts understand these problems and also how they alleviate them through interpretation. It is beyond the scope of this chapter to focus on sexual relations other than heterosexual genital intercourse. Before stating my conclusions, I shall offer some remarks showing how psychoanalytic insight can help identify personal obstacles standing in the way of eradicating the social evil of sexism. By *sexism* I am referring to the pervasive prejudice against women in our society that is manifest in laws, educational systems, work opportunities and rewards, distributions of power, and all those self-confirming stereotypes that say that men are inherently superior to women and that women must be kept in their "inferior" place.

Psychical Impotence and Frigidity

Nothing will be gained for present purposes by agonizing over strict clinical or descriptive definitions of impotence and frigidity. It is, however, important, for reasons that will emerge, to avoid importing into one's definitions presuppositions about ability, capacity, achievement, success, and failure.

In the main, *impotence* refers to the absence or disappearance of an erection or the absence of ejaculation during a man's ostensible attempt to perform the sexual act fully. When used more loosely, *impotence* may also refer to premature or minimal ejaculation and to partial erection, in which descriptive respects the notion of degree of impotence seems to be appropriate. Those instances of impotence that have clear organic etiologies need not concern us on this occasion. Traditionally, the other instances have been said to be psychical, that is, caused by psychological factors.

Freud used the term *psychical impotence* to cover all instances of psychological origin, but also and mainly in a narrowed sense to cover the far more common instances of selective impotence. *Selective impotence* refers to a man's being limited to completing the sexual act with only certain types of women; typically these are "degraded" women in relation to whom the man may exclude tender, affectionate, and respectful feelings. Of these men Freud (1910–12, p. 183) said, "The whole sphere of love . . . remains divided. . . . Where they love they do not desire and where they desire they cannot love." Selective impotence is the form most frequently encountered in clinical practice, particularly if one takes account of the fact that it is observed as an intermittent phenomenon just as often in relation to one woman, perhaps the man's wife, as it is in relation to a type of woman.

Frigidity refers to a woman's lack of sexual desire, ardor, and pleasure in sexual intercourse; it may include conscious aversion to the act. One may speak of degrees of frigidity. Corresponding to the man's difficulties with erection and ejaculation are the woman's vaginal tightness and dryness, which, because they usually occasion pain and fear of pain during intercourse, further decrease her sexual arousal and increase her aversion to the act. The term *frigidity* is used by some to refer to the regular absence of orgasm. What Freud said about psychological impotence in the narrowed sense applies, with appropriate changes, to frigidity: psychological frigidity refers commonly to selective frigidity, whether it be with one type of man or with one man at different times. If nowhere else, this selectivity is likely to be evident in the excited and orgasmic masturbation that is often practised by otherwise frigid women.

Freud (1910–12, p. 182) observed the following of the restricted sexual activity of the selectively impotent man: "It is capricious, easily disturbed, often not properly carried out, and not accompanied by much pleasure." The restricted sexuality of the selectively frigid woman shows the same features.

Through Freud's investigations and those of generations of analysts after him, it has been established that one must take account of a multitude of factors before one may claim to have explained individual cases of impotence and frigidity. Indeed, it may be said that there is no significant aspect of personal development and existence that cannot figure as a condition of, or reason for, these disturbances. Foremost among the factors emphasized by Freud is the unconsciously maintained incestuous significance of the sex act. In cases of impotence and frigidity this significance is enlarged, unduly threatening, and dealt with by splitting one's affectionate and erotic feelings and directing only the latter toward "degraded" or otherwise unsuitable persons. For the man, unconsciously, there is also the interfering influence of the castration anxiety associated with his oedipal rivalry with his father; for the woman, there is in addition, and typically unconsciously, the imagined shameful fact of her castration, her mixture of longing and bitterness with respect to her frustrated wishes to bear her father's children, and her envious, appropriative, or destructive attitude toward her partner's penis. Further, the disturbing influence of exaggerated, unconsciously maintained homosexual attachment to the parent of the same sex— the inverse or negative Oedipus complex—is often carried into heterosexual relations, rendering them threatening and unsatisfactory. Disruption may stem as well from special concerns with the so-called voyeuristic and exhibitionistic aspects of sexual intimacy. These aspects are usually connected to infantile observations or imaginings of the primal scene, that is, the parental coupling. They are likely to involve fear of, and shame at, exposing or viewing sexual excitement and confronting the imagined damage and threatening potential of the female genitalia.

But today psychoanalysts realize more than ever that, in addition to oedipal and genital influences, preoedipal or pregenital influences also figure significantly in the heterosexual life of a man or a woman. To the extent that this is so, a person may, for example, view the sex act as devouring and persecutory or excrementally dirty and explosively destructive. Disruption may stem from the imagined and unacceptable requisites of cruelty and suffering in sexual activity. Confusion associated with early and unstable phases of the differentiation of the self (or ego) from others in the environment may be the occasion of one's greatly fearing that one will lose both one's self and one's world through increasing intimacy, mounting sexual excitement, and orgasm.

From one case to the next, the analyst attributes different degrees of importance to these and other, usually unconsciously operative factors. In some cases, one finds that some of these factors may be present with no obvious disruption of sexual performance and no dissatisfaction. In fact, one often finds that for certain people some of the factors are necessary features of sexual performance and satisfaction. In some instances of this kind, such as those involving staged cruelty and suffering, the analyst will speak of perversions. Freud numbered these so-called perverse features among the many "conditions for loving," grouping them thereby with the splitting of feelings and persons that I mentioned earlier. In these instances, the analyst is likely to discern enactments of impotence and frigidity in other areas of life. However, it is more often the case that these "perverse" features retain the status of unconsciously elaborated and repudiated fantasies, and that they act as disturbers of the sexual peace rather than as overt "conditions for loving"; they may also disturb the peace of working and conducting other aspects of one's life. In many cases the analyst's weaving a web of interpretation of these consciously repudiated perverse fantasies goes a long way toward reducing or eliminating direct impotence and frigidity and displaced or symbolic versions of them in work and elsewhere.

Before concluding this introductory survey, I must mention two more sets of common observations. First, many men and women carry through the sexual act on the strength of conscious fantasies they construct during its performance. Typically these fantasies involve someone other than one's actual partner and sometimes they exclude the self as well, or instead. Also, these fantasies often represent relations that are not copulatory and may not even be sexual by ordinary standards; for example, threatening or adventurous interactions or situations may serve the purpose. And the fantasy during heterosexual activity may be homosexual. Recourse to fantasy as a condition for sexual loving is so common that one may hesitate to speak of it as merely disguising impotence or frigidity; but so long as one is clear that these labels are being used with respect to an ideal reference point, and that this reference point is often enough an actual part of human experience and regularly includes extremely satisfying features, there is nothing wrong with this usage. This ideal, of course, is total involvement in the immediate personal relationship, that is, in the actual erotic and affectionate interactions through which it is manifest. This is what psychoanalysts mean by *genitality*. With reference to the ideal of genitality, intercourse based on conscious fantasies falls closer to masturbation than to loving sexual relations. Also short of the ideal are the many instances of sexual intercourse that are simply not very satisfying; it is not unusual for men and women to feel pent up and to masturbate after "completing" these sex acts, as if having to meet their conditions for loving in the isolation of fantasy after the act rather than in the physical closeness during it.

The second addendum is this: on close analysis it often emerges that the actions of one's partner have been playing a key role in one's own impotence or frigidity. What has been getting in the way may be some subtly conveyed lack of ardor or tenderness or some aversion or rage. But the analyst will not be content to stop asking questions once a strong case has been made for the existence of this kind of disturbing factor. The analyst will go on to try to understand why the analysand has chosen and stayed with that kind of sexual partner or why he or she has refrained from taking steps to improve the situation. Relationships of this kind are unconsciously imbued with meaning of many kinds; typically they serve certain purposes rather than being plain bad luck. To the extent that this is so, the actions of one's sexual partner imply actions of one's own. As a rule, it takes two to make a chronic sexual problem. However, what will be decisive finally is not the partner's overt behavior in itself, but the way it fits and confirms the analysand's unconsciously maintained infantile imagoes, such as that of the abandoning mother or prohibiting father. In this light, the relational sexual problem gets to be seen as a route to what is centrally and anciently conflictual for the individual; and following that route will be the best way to alleviate that problem, for it will rest on a frank reconsideration of one's lifelong human predicaments rather than on the technological adjustments of one's sexual output that may be effected by other forms of therapy.

Ascriptions of Agency and Sexist Terminology

At this point, we may begin to consider the inter-related themes of action and sexism by examining the extended connotations of the words *impotence* and *frigidity*. *Impotence* means lacking in strength, force, drive, or power; it is a word specifically suited to describing a person as agent. *Frigidity* means extreme coldness; it is a word specifically suited for describing a milieu. Together the words entail the proposition that in sexual relations a man is acting in a milieu. It is implied that there is only one agent. Although a milieu may be said to have effects, it cannot be said to act. Only people act. It follows from this pair of designations that the woman is by nature an inactive or passive object: if frigid, she is an unsuitable object; if ardent, she is a suitable object. Strength, force, drive, and power are not for her; nor are intent, initiative, interaction, and control. And in the same vein, the properties of milieu are held to be alien to the man's nature.

We may view these implied distinctions under the aspect of figure and ground. According to the conventional terminology for sexual performances, the man—especially his penis—is the figure in the sexual act; the woman—especially her vagina—is the ground. In figure-ground relationships, it is the ground that sets off the figure and never the other way around; unless, of course, it is a case of a reversible figure-ground configuration, in which respect fixed designations of figure and ground make no sense. The figure imparts some properties to the ground; visually a gray ground becomes whiter if it contains a very dark figure and blacker if it contains a very light figure. It is also possible to say that the ground imparts some properties to the figure; for instance, a dark ground makes a light figure look whiter and a light ground makes a light figure look darker. Thus reciprocal influences are exerted by figure and ground. But this kind of reciprocity does not obviate the fact that one is figure and the other ground. According to the world picture established by the words *impotence* and *frigidity,* a man may arouse a woman sexually without thereby establishing her as a figure in the sexual act and certainly not as *the* figure of the act; instead, he will have changed the temperature of his milieu, and it will be a change that sets him off all the more as figure through his enhanced and confirmed potency. A man's anxiously striving to bring his partner to orgasm often has less to do with concern for her as a person and more with self-centered confirmation of his being the potent figure or agent acting on an object. Sometimes men use impregnation for the same kind of self-reassurance.

The figure has definition, boundaries, articulation, structure, prominence, and impact—it is that which is seen as such; it is what is looked at; it shows itself by standing out; it is remembered. The ground or milieu is amorphous, unbounded, unarticulated, unstructured —it is seen only through what it does for or to the figure; it is necessary for the sake of something else; it is modest, recessive, anonymous, set back or behind; it is not remembered, at least not for itself. In this connection, Virginia Woolf likened the woman to the flattering mirror that shows off the man.

It is obvious that the sexist idea of what it is woman's nature to be and what she ought to be, if she is to be feminine, corresponds closely to the correlated terms *milieu, object,* and *ground.* And it is equally obvious that this correspondence is greatest or most blatant in the realm of sexual activity. This sexist idea is shared by the mass of men and women and it covers much of the conventional role of motherhood as well. Typically, male chauvinism or phallocentrism is the condition of both sexes, even if not equally so in every respect. When I say *sexist,* therefore, I am not referring only to men; nor am I referring only to its crudest forms. Elsewhere (Schafer, 1974), I have tried to show how sexist thinking influenced Freud's formulation of his profound insights into the psychology of women.

The ground receives and incorporates the figure; the figure intrusively occupies the ground. The woman receives the man who intrudes into her. As the child is told, Daddy plants the seed in Mommy. The man has sexual drive; the woman sexual appetite. Consequently, the woman who assumes the prerogatives of the figure, as conventionally described, can expect to be viewed as masculine or as hostile to men or competitive with them. In psychoanalytic work, one often observes that, unconsciously, a woman of this sort is in fact attempting to depose the ruling man and be a man herself, and, more specifically, to acquire symbolically a penis for herself by taking it away from the man. One familiar clinical instance of seizing the conventional male prerogative is encountered in the sexually tantalizing, exhibitionistic, but frigid woman who, unconsciously and totally, equates her body and its sexual prominence and influence with the phallus.

Vagina Dentata and Phallus as Breast

The fantasy, shared by men and women alike, of the *vagina dentata*—the mutilating, castrating, devouring, vaginal mouth—is frequently found to play a major part in impotence and frigidity. In the man's case, the fantasy of being unmanned by this vagina is in large part a way of wishfully projecting that he wishes to turn into a woman, for men envy women, too; in the fantasy, the frightening female organ will do to him what he secretly wishes to bring about, while yet fearing that outcome. Alternatively, the *vagina dentata* fantasy may be the man's way of regressively retreating to the imagined ultimate milieu—the mother's womb or the postnatal, pregenital configuration of the mother's holding arms and lap, nourishing breast, and smiling face. By such imaginings, the man hopes to merge into the ground and become one with the passive object. Thereby he will exist only through or in an indefinite other; no longer will he be required to be a person in his own right or to deal with another figure in its own right. Perhaps thereby he will also avoid that brute annihilation of the woman which he unconsciously believes to be the consequence of his being the necessarily rapacious figure in the sexual relation.

On the woman's part, the *vagina dentata* fantasy is a typical correlate of the unconsciously maintained fantasy that she has been wronged and humiliated by having been denied a penis or of having had it taken away from her, and of her having accordingly adopted an envious, rivalrous, castrating attitude toward the phallic, rapacious man. Implied in this retaliatory orientation is her wishing to become a figure or an agent or to re-

gain that status. She wishes to be a figure with definition, structure, visibility—someone who counts as a
person. But at the same time, in one of those unconsciously conflictual or paradoxical actions, her dentali-
zation of the vagina may well also imply a regressive
movement, specifically a returning to the role of the
biting infant at the breast.

Psychoanalysts have defined a widespread, if not uni-
versal, fantasy in which, unconsciously, penis and breast
are equated; and correlatively, semen and milk. These
equations stand out in the analyses of those people who
have centered their sexual interest on fellatio fantasies
and practices, no matter whether they have done so in
an overexcited, repulsed, or paralyzed fashion. Much
gagging and vomiting of psychological origin can be
attributed to a person's engaging in these fantasies conflictually and unconsciously.

Think what this equation of breast and phallus implies. The shadow of the mother has fallen on the
phallus, and on the man whose organ it is; accordingly,
the sexual act is, unconsciously, bisexual, and it is oral
as well as genital. The equation of breast and phallus
also implies that those who view sexism and phallocentrism as synonymous are oversimplifying the psychological state of affairs. The bodily presence or absence
of the phallus as phallus is only one part of the story.
Today, psychoanalysts would generally agree that the
breast-phallus equation is a lasting monument to the
influence of the mother who necessarily both feeds and
deprives. But if this is so, then figure-ground relations
start at the breast and to a considerable extent remain
there. It serves the defensive needs of both sexes to

deny this fact, and it has served the defensive and con-
formist needs of many psychoanalysts of both sexes to
minimize or deny this primacy. I shall return to this
point shortly.

In one of his last major contributions to the topic of
femininity, Freud (1933) finally acknowledged the enduring primacy of this maternal figure in the lives of
women, though he did so only in a limited context.
He did so when he ascribed many of the difficulties
women have with their husbands to their importing
into their marital relationships unresolved problems
with their mothers; not just that they are identified
with their troubled mothers, but that they unconsciously set their husbands up as unsatisfactory mothers. One might say in this respect that they establish
maternal transferences to their husbands. Had Freud
taken a more general view of the matter, he might have
gone on to emphasize the positive potential of this
same transference. A woman can, and often does, find
a good mother as well as a good man and father in her
husband, and to that extent has a richer and more
gratifying relationship with him. Carrying this line of
thought a step further—a step warranted by clinical
observation—a man's integrated identification with
some kind of good-mother image contributes to the
warmth, generosity, and stability of his heterosexual
relationships; the intent of this kind of female identification is not primarily self-castration.

Sexism, whether blatant or unconsciously insidious,
denies these insights and opportunities to men and
women. Even more so does it deny the paternal potential in a woman's being the figure in relation to a man.

One finds little or no reference to this factor in the psychoanalytic literature. Most analysts seem to be content to stop at the idea of the phallic woman as *woman:* they view that imagined figure primarily in relation to castration anxiety; they dwell on people's unconsciously needing to reassure themselves that there is no anatomical difference between the sexes and thus no imagined castration to fear and no irreparable genital damage or deprivation to come to terms with. But, crucial as it may be, this is too narrow a view of the matter, for the phallic woman also contains the fantasized and perceived paternal potency, authority, and personhood. Insofar as a woman's activity and authority is unconsciously portrayed as masculine or phallic, it implies the father's potency in action. In relation to this potency, a man becomes unconsciously passive, objectified, feminized. As I mentioned, for him this is a consummation devoutly to be wished as well as feared, and so feared all the more.

The Subjugation of the Mother

In considering impotence, frigidity, and sexism, one cannot overestimate the significance of the infantile fantasies of the phallic and paternal mother and the *vagina dentata.* Of equal importance are the mutual envy that exists between the sexes with its correlated wishing for and fearing the imagined castrated status. These contradictory representations and orientations pervade unconscious fantasizing. But the first phase of psychological development involves other great problems that contribute to the development of the personal and social issues with which we are here concerned. One in particular is the difficult, stressful, and unstable differentiation of oneself as an active figure—a person—in relation to the caretaking and terribly powerful maternal figure. Through reconstructive analysis of dreams and transferences, which is paralleled by psychoanalytic child observation, it appears to be the case that the young child imagines loss of individuation to be a kind of devouring engulfment or annihilation that is perpetrated either by the mother or on the mother—a fantasy that, paradoxically, and like the castration fantasy, is experienced both excitedly and with shuddering horror.

This archaically conceived struggle for and against individuation seems to remain a lifelong project. Although some people continue this struggle more conspicuously, erratically, and anxiously than others, the fact of the struggle must be taken into account in any effort to understand problems of gender identification and the role of gender identification in relations between the sexes.

In the case of girls there is the later problem—it was first to have been securely established in psychoanalytic interpretation—of the struggle she carries on anxiously and guiltily against her rivalrous oedipal identification with her mother; this is the identification by means of which the girl hopes, unconsciously though often also consciously, to take the mother's place with the father. This later problem appears differently in the case of the boy: for him it is necessary to devalue the oedipal mother as one way of moderating his desiring to win her and his fearing that he will be inadequate to the task of winning her or satisfying her sexually. For the girl and boy alike, and both preoedipally and oedipally, the mother, far from being the ground or the passive object, emerges experientially as a gigantic figure to contend with and come to terms with. Speaking of the problems of the female writer in *A Room of One's Own*, Virginia Woolf recognized this phenomenon when she said, "A woman writing thinks back through her mothers." She would not have been wrong to say this of anyone, whether they are eating, dressing, loving, or giving lectures.

One of the important vantage points for viewing our analytic data, then, is the one that looks squarely at the developing person's struggle for individuation and for an independent sense of adequacy, wholeness, safety, and worth. In this struggle, it seems that the imposing figure of the mother, which is the prime representative of womanhood, must be cut down or cut up. This figure must be rejected, derogated, set apart, or consciously ignored. Here then is a set of powerful reasons why both men and women are ready to participate in the socially reinforced discrimination against women, or at least to assent to it passively. For the same reasons, this figure must be protected or repaired with special care—often by idealization.

Critics of our sexist society find much to support their position in the fact that many or most mothers have more or less accommodated themselves to this state of affairs: these are women who have given up aspirations of their own other than serving as a favorable ground or flattering mirrors for their husbands and children; they have neglected their own competences and potentialities of other sorts; they are disillusioned and discouraging figures who depend on defensive idealizations of them for self-esteem. Today, many thoughtful young women scorn their conventionally sexist mothers and women of their sort. They regard them as wives who have declined into domesticity. They are disturbed, unconsciously even more than consciously, by their inevitable identification with these mothers. Although they seek desperately to escape, deny, or cancel out this identification, they make the effort so totalistically that they do so in vain, achieving rather a radical discontinuity in their sense of themselves. Moreover they cannot grasp the full meaning of that attempt at disidentification, unless they take into account the problems, dating from infancy, of individuating from the archaic mother figure and establishing a two-person relationship with her; they must also take into account the problems posed by the oedipal mother imago and the disillusioning mother imago of later phases of psychosexual development.

Thus, even as a demoralizing figure, the mother is still maintained as a forceful presence in one's own life. She is a figure to be reckoned with in one's subjective "inner world." The subjugation of women, in which women play a part that is more complex than that assigned in simple feminist theories of social reinforcement, is centrally the subjugation of the powerful mother figure of childhood. Unconsciously, it can get to seem that one's life depends on the subjugation, and the social world seems organized to lend its support to that project.

It is not sexist, as some radical feminists claim, to

spell out and work with these insights into the relations between the sexes. It is sexist to maintain that the disruptive dramatization and proliferation of these familiar fantasies are altogether unmodifiable, that is to say, are simply and totally built into human development and have nothing to do with a social reality that encourages and reinforces them in countless ways. It is sexist to think that a girl would naturally feel inferior and envious simply because she lacks a penis. It is sexist to say that nothing can be done about the reinforcing social reality, and even more so to assert that nothing should be done about it. Those feminists who have been making the developmental and social distinctions I am making are, I think, in a better position to attack the societal and therapeutic problem, for they have a more intimate knowledge of the enemy.

The Whole Person

To get any further with the discussion we must consider next what it means to be a whole person, and do so from the standpoint of action theory and the action language that is its manifestation. I shall be referring now to an ideal definition, recognizing that in life we approach or realize our ideals only intermittently, though some of us are further along in this respect than others. One of the fruits of effective personal psychoanalysis is that one affirms this ideal and on the average lives closer to it than before one's analysis.

A whole person is the one who acts, the agent. A whole person acts without profound reservations about the fact of acting, and so acts with presence and per-

sonal authority and without anxiously introducing serious disclaimers—such as the claim that one is passively
moved by natural forces, by one's mind or one's split-
off self. In sexual relations, as elsewhere, a person acts
on others who, by that very fact, become that person's
objects or ground or milieu. But this is still too narrow
a view of the matter, and potentially too sexist a view,
for a whole person also refuses to deny personhood to
others. Psychologically, there cannot be only one whole
person in the world; those who engage in extreme fantasies of omnipotence, such as paranoiac patients, implicitly sacrifice their own personal wholeness in doing
so. Those who are thoroughly egocentric make the
same sacrifice.

Guaranteeing the personal wholeness of others entails a readiness on one's own part to serve on numer-
ous occasions as object, ground, or milieu in relation
to them, for they, too, must be given scope to exercise
and confirm *their* personal wholeness. A good conversation exemplifies what I am referring to: can there be
good conversation with only one person communicat-
ing in words, sounds, and gestures? Here we reencoun-
ter the phenomenon—I will not say analogy—of the
reversible figure-ground relationship, and we come to
the problem of changing the terms in which we understand the relations between the sexes.

We know that adamant rebellion does not change
the terms of a problem with authority; the terms remain the same except that they have now a minus sign
placed before them. Nor does a rigid role reversal
change the terms of a problem: the miser who becomes
a spendthrift, the mouse who becomes a lion, the ho-

mosexual woman who acts more like the stereotypical
man than most men and the homosexual man who acts
more like the stereotypical woman than most women—
none of these has changed the terms of the problem.
Each is attempting to achieve what has been called in
psychoanalytic discussion a change of content without
a change of structure. A flip-flop is only a change of
content; it accepts the structure of things as they are.
Money, majesty, or macho remain the important struc-
turing factors. Analysts have learned to be wary of such
changes when, as often happens, they observe analysands abruptly and dramatically reversing their characteristic patterns of manifest action.

A fundamental change of the terms in which a problem is defined is a structural change. With regard to
sexism, however, the change of terms that is called for
is not limited to changing by conscious decision alone
that which is to be designated *masculine* and *feminine*
or *active* and *passive;* nor is it limited to consciously
reallocating the prerogatives of the two sexes. Changes
in both of these respects, though terribly important
and possible, depend for their force on a necessary and
consequential change in the idea of a whole person.

A whole person, I suggest, may be described as a reversible set of actions and modes of action in the respects I have been describing. A whole person allows
the reversibility, in a relatively conflict-free fashion.
He or she refrains from insisting on being only agent or
object, only figure or ground, only active or passive, or
only masculine or feminine, as conventionally defined.
The reversibility is itself a form of action in that refraining and allowing are themselves actions. A whole

person is neither threatened by reversibility nor incapable of enjoying either position in a relationship. The mutuality or reversibility of being a person not only matters more to a whole person than conventional ascriptions of masculine-feminine and active-passive; to a considerable extent, adopting the idea of persons-in-relation renders the other ideas unwelcome interferences in the business of living. The reversibility includes projecting the other side of one's bisexuality into one's partner and enjoying it there: the man projecting what he regards as his feminine side and vice versa. That the change of terms is fundamental will be evident not so much by what one says but by how one lives one's life and how one understands it.

It must also be remarked that the reversibility, once established securely, no longer entails the threat or experience of loss of personhood. The reversible figure-ground model implies different and concurrent modes of agency: the tension between the alternating figures is essential to the phenomenon.

None of what I am saying discounts differences in degree and style of reversibility; to state an ideal is not to prescribe absolute uniformity in its realization. To those who would cry, *"Vive la difference!"*, thinking of the pleasures of heterosexuality, I can only point out that nothing in my argument minimizes the different and complementary conformations, roles and and pleasure possibilities of male and female bodies; if anything, my argument goes some way toward enhancing the possibilities of loving unanxiously, unconflictually, and without drastic confusion of stereotyped roles.

Consider, for example, the burden of always being

pleasing, which weighs on most women in our sexist
world and contributes to their masochistic and depres-
sive proclivities. This burden of being a reassuring
milieu first and foremost can be lifted and replaced by
the pleasurable option, open to both sexes, of pleasing
others of either sex—and of displeasing them, too,
when it is in a good cause. A change of this sort—not a
change to unmitigated hostility—will be terribly difficult to achieve. This is so because, among other things,
it means coming to terms with the incorporated, terribly powerful mother of infancy and of the oedipal
period; this is the figure who ordinarily is felt to be
hidden and controlled behind the ready smile and
yielding empathy. For reasons I gave earlier, both men
and women collude in subjugating this archaic mother
—and the sexist environment reinforces this pattern
from the beginning.

Changing Sexual Patterns

We must consider next whether any movement toward the ideal of the whole person implies, as it might
seem to, that henceforth anything goes in the sphere
of physical sexuality; more specifically, whether figure-
ground reversibility implies that overt mass bisexuality
is in the cards. There are grounds for thinking that bisexual experimentation is already on the increase in
our society. But I do not think any forecast or recom-
mendation of that sort follows from what I have been
saying. There is also reason to think that so long as we
continue to have nuclear families in which women
serve as the primary figures of early child care, and

so long as we have a social order characterized by class structure, centralization and impersonalization of power, and unequal distribution of private property, the prevailing pattern of sexual-identity formation and sexual relations will remain difficult to change radically. Personally, I do not know what kind of people would inhabit a world that retained none of these features, and I am not persuaded by utopian manifestoes that anyone else knows. To say this is not to endorse the social order as it is; nor is it to speak of bisexuality or homosexuality as social evils we must do everything to prevent or stamp out: it is only to begin speaking to the question of what would result from any significant change in the idea of being a person and the importance accorded this change. Given both the archaic fantasies of the child and our present social order, it may even be that widespread change of the sort I have suggested is not possible. But change relative to the ideal of the whole person does commonly take place during personal psychoanalysis, and so I think that a psychoanalyst may venture to say something on this question without being recklessly visionary.

I would expect the change to be of two sorts. I already mentioned one—the enhancement of all aspects of heterosexual relationships. The other change would be, not a radical increase in the incidence of bisexuality, but rather a freeing and enrichment of social relations between members of the same sex. Intense same-sex friendships would thrive to the extent that the value-laden and anxiety-laden categories masculine-feminine and active-passive recede in importance, for to that extent the limited intrusion of sexual feeling

into same-sex relationships would be more easily accepted as constituent elements of being a person and
of loving relations between persons. It would be regulated more easily, because less anxiously and guiltily,
and it would not be tied to the notion that one must
now go all the way with it. As present, the prospect of
homosexual feeling holds great terror for most people,
and so it sets great limits on their relationships with
others of the same sex. The often troubled relations
between son and father, mother and daughter, brother
and brother, sister and sister, would stand to gain much
from a reduction of these limits.

I know, of course, that intense same-sex friendships
are not rare in this sexist world, but I would point out
that more often than not immersion in these friendships implies a relative deemphasis of heterosexual relationships. Where being a whole person is the primary
value, neither kind of relationship would interfere with
the other as seriously as they now usually do. One sees
that this is so when personal psychoanalysis has been
carried through effectively: then the analysand's either-
or approach to human relationships and personal emotionality, both within and between the sexes, is usually
radically diminished. Beyond the changed understanding and valuation of what is embraced by the terms
masculine and *feminine,* and *active* and *passive,* there
is ideally a changed idea and an increased importance
of being a whole person in relation to other persons.

"Good," "Bad," "Can," and "Can't"

Some other changes in the terms of the problems of
sexuality and sexism that can be accomplished through

psychoanalysis concern the idea of the good and the bad, the innocent and the guilty, the safe and the dangerous; under a different and crucial aspect, these changes concern the idea of success and failure. The proper understanding of these changes depends on an action theory of persons.

Modification of the idea of the good and the bad, the innocent and the guilty, and the safe and the dangerous can for the most part be subsumed under the traditional psychoanalytic heading of modification of the superego. This modification relieves the ego of the pressure to be as defensive as it may get to be in relation to the varieties of sexual desiring and other action. This is a familiar and crucially important chapter of psychoanalysis and does not need a detailed summary here. Suffice it to say that the analysand may come to accept that it is an inescapable part of being a whole person to continue being in some measure an orally receptive and biting baby, an anally sensuous and dirty baby, and a bisexually incestuous young child who is identified with both parents and desires each of them erotically. Through analysis, these continuities may get to be seen as the inescapable heritage of growing up human, which means developing into a person in the context of a family and a society composed of men and women. It also means growing up with a male or female body that has its own pleasure possibilities and vulnerabilities; moreover, it means reclaiming one's body as one's own and asserting the right to decide on its uses in sexual relationships. This set of modifications typically has the effect of reducing the unconsciously maintained dominance of many of the infantile carryovers that have been most disturbing in one's relations with one's partner. These carryovers have remained that disturbing because they have been most anxiously, guiltily, and uncompromisingly fragmented and repudiated.

In this respect, subjective liberation is civilizing. Through psychoanalysis, what once could only be desperate adventures, engaged in surreptitiously or in fantasy or else sternly prohibited, now become possibilities of play. The sexual act as a whole becomes a possibility of play. The claim that this is so is in no way incompatible with the claim that sexual loving is also a possibility of intimacy of the most serious kind. Play and seriousness are themselves freed from the trap of either-or judgments. These either-or judgments bear the mark of one's own archaic, unconsciously enforced moral categories—one's superego, so-called. This "superego" enforcement is frequently increased in scope and severity upon marrying, having children, or reaching middle age, for these are transitional actions and happenings in connection with which people often consolidate further their archaic identifications with prohibiting parental imagoes. If these imagoes are particularly forbidding, problems of impotence and frigidity may increase from then on, and so may sexist attitudes.

Changing the idea of success and failure at sex—the idea of making it or not making it—comes under another aspect than modification of "superego" identifications. What it requires is a new appreciation that, in the most fundamental psychological sense, impotence and frigidity are not failures at all. Here we arrive at the importance of correcting presuppositions that we are dealing, not with actions, but with abilities, capacities, or achievements—with cans and can'ts. Like other symptoms, impotence and frigidity are more correctly and profitably regarded as complex actions corresponding to complex situations. Even though their final manifestations are physical and physiological states of muscular, circulatory, and secretory unpreparedness for the complex sex act, these manifestations are appropriate features of the intentional actions and situations they unconsciously imply. They are not happenings— events to be suffered passively.

To put what I mean concretely: if, for example, unconsciously, one partner in a marital sex act is fleeing a scene of incestuous sexuality, that person is neither in a marital sexual situation or moving more deeply into it, nor is anything happening to a passive victim: unconsciously, that person is fleeing. Similarly, if, unconsciously, one partner in a sex act is tightening up mentally and muscularly in order to avoid an orgasmic anal explosion, an imagined eventuality that will make a mess or be destructive and in either case threaten loss of love and painful shame, that person is not to any appreciable degree interacting erotically and genitally with another person; nor is that person an unfortunate passive object: unconsciously, that person is holding in. And if, to give one more example, one is doing all one can not to show oneself off or see the other, owing to the still influential prohibitions or shame connected with infantile exhibitionism and voyeurism, then one is hiding one's body and one's excitement, or one is blinding oneself or imaginally turning one's back on one's lover, and in either case hardly qualifying as a lover

oneself: far from finding oneself out of it, one is uncon-
ciously making sure to be out of it.

Whatever the explanation, it is psychologically
wrong to speak of failure. In the psychoanalytic redescription, the impotent or frigid person is doing
exactly what it is right to do under the unconsciously
defined, fantasized circumstances that count the most.
From the standpoint of psychic reality, one might even
call impotence and frigidity successes, were it not for
the fact that success also no longer seems to be the right
sort of word. We are simply dealing with actions carried
through for what they are to the agent. Once they are
sufficiently understood, there is no plausible alternative. The idea of failure makes sense only with respect
to some conscious and inaccurate idea about what kind
of situation one is in and what one wishes to do in it.
That limited conscious view precludes insightful
change.

In contrast, the implicit or explicit action view makes
insightful change possible—change, not success, change
through recasting the fundamental terms of the problem. To accomplish any such change, it will be necessary to overcome or mitigate the societal seduction of
boys into uneasy representatives of pure masculine
force and of girls into demoralized representatives of
pure feminine milieu. Here is a start on a social psychological theory of seduction of children that can replace
the theory which Freud once entertained and then
mostly rejected, that is, the theory of physical seduction
of children who later became neurotic. The psychological theory would, however, have to take account of
what psychoanalysis has established, namely, the eager-

ness with which children participate in these categorial seductions owing to the thrilling and terrifying features of their infantile fantasy life. In the light of this new seduction theory, we may hope to reclaim many disclaimed actions in the interest of helping people be whole, responsible, reciprocally related persons. That kind of reclamation work can only enhance pleasurable, consummated sexual relations.

Afterword
ACTION LANGUAGE—AN ALTERNATIVE TO METAPSYCHOLOGY

In *A New Language for Psychoanalysis* (1976), I presented action language as an alternative to Freudian metapsychology. Action language is my adaptation of certain theses that have been put forward by various twentieth-century thinkers concerned with the philosophy of mind, action, existence, persons, and interpretation. This adaptation is neither more nor less philosophical than metapsychology. This is so because Freud, in developing metapsychology, was adapting certain lines of argument concerning the philosophy of mind and science that were being advanced in his day. Freud underestimated and so understated the extent to which his attempts to develop a general theory of mind ("the mental apparatus") were philosophical projects.

In calling action language a new language for psychoanalysis, I took the stand that the words *metapsychological* and *psychoanalytic* should not be regarded as synonymous. I argued that psychoanalytic theory must be viewed from the standpoint of systematic language rules, and I set forth the principal rules of the new action language. Once metapsychology is no longer equated with psychoanalysis, one must face the difficult question, What is distinctively psychoanalytic about psychoanalysis?

I also referred to action language as the native tongue of psychoanalysis. In this respect I claimed that action language clarifies the often implicit strategy of clinical psychoanalytic interpretation. This clarification is particularly important in connection with the interpretation of fantasy activity carried on unconsciously and conflictually. Language and insight are inseparable, and on this premise I tried to show that action language comes closer by far than metapsychology ever could to capturing the essential changes brought about through psychoanalysis. These are the changes that are both manifest in and based on genuine, integrated, insightful reconsideration of one's life, one's problems, and one's options.

It is not paradoxical to call action language both new and native, for my point is that there has always been something right under the analytic nose that has not been recognized, appreciated, and conceptualized systematically.

I emphasize especially the strategy of interpretation and the inseparability of language and insight. I do so on the ground that the theoretical language of psychoanalysis should be organically related to the classical interpretive method of adult analysis and to the data generated by this method. Psychoanalysis is an interpretive discipline. It works toward and through insight. This being the case, its nature can only be obscured by the adoption of a preestablished metatheory based on mechanistic concepts far removed from practice, which is the kind of metatheory that metapsychology stems from. As an interpretive discipline, psychoanalysis requires instead a rigorous account of how to state its data and the form and content of its interpretations in a way that is systematic and set at the least possible distance from the clinical situation. Psychoanalysts should develop no more theory than they need for their method. What is appropriate is not so much an ambitious, all-encompassing theory of mind as a modest empirical theory of how to name and interpret the human activity that is, in keeping with certain rules, observed and inferred during the psychoanalytic process. In other words, the first order of business is to develop a data language that lends itself to progressively more general or higher-order redescriptions; these will be redescriptions that both state and organize the actions that make up the analytic hour. Most analysts have, however, followed Freud in attempting to develop psychoanalysis as a general psychology or an all-encompassing theory of personality development, and so have committed themselves to psychobiological, child-developmental, and other principles which do not find their empirical support in the psychoanalytic situation.

The plan of presentation is the following. I shall give an abbreviated version of the account of action language that was presented in *A New Language for Psychoanalysis*. In addition to synopsizing, I shall dwell on certain points, such as excessive claiming of action and the relation of action to bodily factors, that appear to have presented special difficulty to some readers of the earlier volume. I shall prepare the ground for this synopsis by taking up, first, a decisive feature of personal change during beningly influential psychoanalyses, and, second, a decisive feature of the strategy of psychoanalytic interpretation. Then, the abbreviated account of action language, to be followed by a concise statement of what may be taken to be the central regulatory principles of Freudian interpretation. To some readers, this concluding summary statement will sound so obvious and workaday that it will seem not theoretical at all. My claim, however, is that the statement in question is based on a necessary change of

perspective on theory itself rather than on any suspension or narrowing of theoretical interest.

Personal Change during Psychoanalysis

The importance of discussing the nature of personal
change during analysis lies in a familiar methodological assumption, namely, that from regularly observed
directions of change during the analytic work one may
infer essential features of that work itself. By essential
features of the work I am referring chiefly to certain
fundamental messages conveyed through free association and interpretation; most of all I am referring to
those messages that retain a constant point of reference
through all the well-known variations in the content of
what is being brought up, pointed out, or integrated
insightfully.

In taking up personal change I shall not be reviewing
the familiar descriptions that have been formulated
from the various metapsychological points of view: the
dynamic point of view (e.g., the reduction and modification of unconscious infantile conflict); the genetic
point of view (e.g., the progression toward postambiva-
lent genitality); the topographic point of view (e.g., the
expansion of consciousness at the expense of the repressed unconscious); the structural view (e.g., the extension of the domain of the mature ego at the expense
of the id, the archaic superego, and the infantile danger
situations and defenses); the adaptive point of view
(e.g., increasing the autonomy of ego functions and
promoting the effectiveness of the ego's synthetic function and the testing of inner as well as external reality);

and the economic point of view (e.g., increased supplies of relatively neutralized libido and aggression and the ego's increased capacity for such neutralization). Nor shall I be summarizing what has been added in recent years concerning such variables as identification with the analyst's organizing functions, separation-individuation, object constancy, mature forms of narcissism, and cohesiveness of the self. Some of these considerations may be subsumed under one or more of the traditional metapsychological points of view, while others, though couched in metapsychological language, may be shown to require the development of alternative theoretical languages.

I do not question that these varied perspectives on change are appropriate and justified so long as one is using metapsychology or is avowedly developing some alternative to it. I emphasize only that these perspectives on change refer to an abundance of data on different levels of abstraction, and that these are data of which some kind of account must be given by any psychoanalyst. An alternative to metapsychology must therefore provide another coherent way to talking about these same data. For example, one must provide such a way of talking about what has been called unconscious conflict, the superego, the vicissitudes of self- and object representations, neutralization, and particularly the crucial position of bodily fantasy in mental activity. But an alternative theory and its language is not to be confused with the raw words, gestures, and figurative speech of the analytic hour. For example, if someone says "my inner self," the analyst, in turn, is not obliged to speak of "inner," "self," or "inner self" in theoretical propositions. The theoretical problem is how best to render, organize, and generalize these lowest-order data that are highlighted by the psycho-analytic method.

One constant point of reference marks the process of change through which these data are manifest: the analysand progressively recognizes, accepts, revises, refines, and lives in terms of the idea of the self as agent. This is to say that, in one way or another and more and more, the analysand sees himself or herself as being the person who essentially has been doing the things from which he or she was apparently suffering upon entering analysis, and from many other problems as well that will have been defined only during the analysis itself. For example, it is established progressively that it is the analysand who has been fragmenting or splitting by repressing, projecting, and adopting other defensive measures; who has been arranging his or her life so that it has been a series of sexual, social, occupational, financial, or creative failures or traumata; who has been engaging in wishful thinking and rationalizing; and who has been tenaciously and unconsciously insisting on intermingled and conflictual oral, anal, and phallic views of human existence. Increasingly, the analysand claims or reclaims as his or her actions what was previously disclaimed.

The opposite extreme of excessive disclaiming is excessive claiming. Analysis also establishes progressively that it is the analysand who, unconsciously and painfully, has been arbitrarily but understandably assuming responsibility for both the fortunate and unfortunate happenings of life. By the term *happenings* I am referring to those events over which in actuality the analysand as child or adult had little or no control. Conceptually, happening is the alternative to action. The category of happenings may include major illnesses and physical defects, accidents, early parental neglect or abuse, and deaths and other losses, as well as special actual advantages, privileges, and opportunities. Unconsciously, if not consciously, children take upon themselves the responsibility for these happenings.

Analytic insight always deals with an extended continuum of claiming and disclaiming. The analysand appears to have been engaged in both too much false claiming of action and too much false disclaiming of action. The desirable direction of change in personal psychoanalysis is the analytically convincing moderation of these excesses. Without this change, insight into specific content lacks meaning and effect.

This point may be put in other terms. The analysand learns about the history of his or her unconsciously elaborated psychic reality, recognized now for what it is. Psychic reality is interpreted as the construction the analysand has been putting on actual and imagined situations and events in the course of his or her life. In the analysis, these constructions are defined through close study particularly of the transference and resistance. This history of psychic reality amounts to a special kind of narrative—what may be called *the psychoanalytic life history* (see lecture 1). Far from being a static arrangement of archeological deposits, this life history is shown to be always an actively utilized, though self-contradictory or conflictual, strategy for defining and acting in one's current subjective situa-

tion. That is to say, it is a certain kind of incoherent
or compromised history that one has been telling oneself or that has been implied in the view one has been
taking of oneself in one's total life situation. And it is
the self-defeating policies and practices one has adopted
and has been following on the basis of that life-historical
account. I emphasize that for psychoanalysis, one *tells*
a history; one does not *have* a history. It is a history of
something, however; a fabrication won't do. In this
history, the past and the present mutually define one
another in a complex manner.

But it is not only the unconsciously elaborated fantasy content of this life history that undergoes change.
More important is the change that is wrought in the
way this history is organized, and this change is a correlate of the analysand's recognition that he or she has
been the imperfect, biased, censorious, revisionist historian of this life. To characterize this change as an
altered mode of telling as well as an altered content of
what is told is to give another account—an action account—of a major aspect of what psychoanalysts are
used to calling structural change or change in the ego's
intersystemic and intrasystemic relations.

The Strategy of Interpretation

The other facet of the psychoanalytic process that it
is necessary to discuss before turning to action language
itself is a decisive feature of the strategy of interpretation. In characterizing the constant point of reference
for describing the way people change during analysis,
I have already indicated what this feature is. My point

is that the analysand is progressively discovering, and the analyst is progressively making it plain to the analysand, not only *that* but *how* he or she is the agent or is not the agent of both the problems for which analysis was initially sought and all the other problems that are being defined. The analysand's ascriptions of agency are reviewed, sorted out, revised, and reorganized; often, they are organized for the first time. The analysis demonstrates that the analysand is unconsciously taking this or that view of the psychoanalytic situation and relationship, seeing it, say, as orally depriving, sadomasochistic, homosexually seductive, or narcissistically damaging. However much the analysand initially represents the analytic situation and relationship in falsely passive and falsely active terms, he or she increasingly reenvisions this excessive emphasis on passive and active representations as an interpretable way of looking at things; it is a way that involves strategies of control and defense, gratification, and punishment, and reenactment or repetition. It is not a happening.

In analysis, it is possible to discover how much has always depended on the analysand's having unconsciously adopted certain paradoxical viewpoints with respect to the happenings of his or her life. These viewpoints express infantile psychosexual and aggressive conceptions of existence and the danger situations and archaic self- and object representations corresponding to them. For example, one important problem for the work of analysis is not the bodily fact, taken in itself, whether or not one has a penis, but, in the terms of psychic reality or unconscious fantasy activity, what kinds of psychological facts one has made of this bodily state of affairs at different phases of one's development and how one has perpetuated these varied and conflicting constructions. Although these constructions do reflect the formative and reinforcing influence of parental and other figures, they also enter into the child's interpretations of the actions of these figures, and it is those interpretations that are analyzed rather than exactly reconstructed historical events.

To give an example of another kind, the fact is not simply that one is rigidly defended, but that defense is a form of activity, however passively it may be consciously represented or experienced (Fenichel, 1941). And beyond that fact there is an equally important one brought out earlier by Freud in *Inhibitions, Symptoms and Anxiety* (1926), namely that, unconsciously, the analysand engages in each defensive practice on the basis of fantasizing that gives the sense of the defensive measure and thus is fantasizing that must be analyzed before the defensive practice will be changed. Specifically, Freud mentioned both the unconscious avoidance of touching that is the meaning of the defense of isolation and the fantasized anal blowing away that is the meaning of the defense of undoing.

According to this strategy of interpretation, repetition is not to be viewed as a regulatory principle of the psychic apparatus which one must experience passively; rather, it is to be seen finally as an enactment or re-enactment of certain wishful, conflictual, and frightening infantile situations, such as the primal scene, that unconsciously have continued to be treated as real and current; consequently, for the analysand, these are situations that seem to warrant a continuation of the same infantile practices, no matter how different in appearance things may be represented consciously. The timelessness of the unconscious and the reality of unconscious fantasy, the indestructibility of the infantile wish and the carrying forward of infantile fixations, conflicts, and danger situations—all these and similar points made by Freud are built into the described strategy of interpretation.

In this connection, I will only mention the important point that the strategy of interpretation includes specifying so far as possible when, why, and with which variations and disguises the analysand engages unconsciously in the actions being interpreted. In explicating this feature of interpretation I am in no way downgrading or systematically excluding from consideration the extensive and varied content of interpretation with which psychoanalysts are well acquainted. *That content is not being called into question.* What is in question is the formalizing and generalizing of that content through language rules. Action language is not a set of empirical psychoanalytic propositions; it is a strategy for stating these propositions clearly and parsimoniously.

There are two additional important points. First, in describing the strategy of interpretation as I do, I am not prescribing the wording of interpretations in clinical work, either deliberately or in effect. Second, in emphasizing the person as agent, I am not prescribing any moralistic assault on the analysand, either deliberately or in effect. My expositions of action language have frequently been misunderstood in both respects. What is being asserted is that interpretation works toward the analysand's recognizing, accepting, refining, and more deliberately applying the idea of self as agent. In the process of change, the analysand is regularly observed to take far more responsibility consciously for some things, and for other things far less. One familiar instance of the latter is what psychoanalysts are used to calling reduction of the influence of the archaic infantile superego. The analysand's sense of responsibility is altered, but this alteration ideally remains what it has always been—the fruit of collaborative insight and shared analytic experience. A genuine change of this sort cannot be imposed by verbal manipulations; nor can it be the result of a demand in any ordinary sense of that word, and certainly not of a moralistic demand.

That we are considering an essential feature of interpretation is evident from the fact that, almost regardless of the analyst's manifest way of wording his or her interventions, so long as those interventions do not fundamentally violate this interpretive strategy and are correct and well timed, analysands who are benefiting from analysis increasingly and appropriately present themselves as agents rather than as passive victims of happenings, be they external circumstance or seemingly autonomous inner forces and fragments of a mind or a self. It becomes no longer defensively important to insist, for example, "My mind is playing tricks on me," "My anger exploded," or "Being a woman has ruined my life." The analysand also modifies and rejects excessive claims; for example, "If I weren't bad and worthless, my parents would have loved me."

The self as agent figures as well in another beneficial change: increased tolerating or enjoying of consciously passive modes of experience. These passive modes finally appear to the analysand under the aspect of what one wants for oneself and engages in rather than as something that threatens to happen to one or from which one is hopelessly blocked off by past experience. Regularly, analysands who initially appear rigid or overcontrolled change in this way. The point I am making now is closely related to what Hartmann (1939) called *adaptive regression* and Kris (1952) called *regression in the service of the ego,* and to what popularly is referred to in such terms as the ability to let go sexually, aggressively, sentimentally, and tenderly.

Action Language

I come now to the review of some of my major language proposals. The metapsychology that is to be replaced presents the person as a mental apparatus within which forces—so-called psychodynamics—and the functions of mental structures are at work, each in its own way. How then shall one speak of such things if, instead of an apparatus of this sort, one takes as one's starting point a person who does things, a being who performs a great variety of actions and performs many of the most important ones unconsciously, archaically, wishfully, repetitively, and conflictually? Obviously, this way of putting the question forecasts its own answer: one describes actions. In doing so, one uses verbs and adverbs to describe the person doing things. One renounces both the use of mentalistic nouns, such as *structure, function, force,* and *drive,* and the use of the adjectives that qualify these nouns, such as *weak, strong, autonomous,* and *rigid.* However, it remains necessary to set forth a more detailed set of proposals together with some clarifying commentary. I emphasize again that these proposals are not technical recommendations, though they do have important technical implications; they concern primarily the language for systemically formulating observation and theory.

1. In action language one speaks of a person performing actions and, when appropriate and useful, of the modes of these actions. Thus, one speaks of a person complying seductively, arguing heatedly, or smiling broadly. One employs verbs and adverbs for this purpose. The raw data of whatever is said and observed is put into the data language of action. One wants to answer the question, "What is this person *doing?*"

2. All mental acts are actions in one or another mode. Thus, a person may remember nostalgically and anticipate apprehensively. On this basis, defensive measures, being mental acts, qualify as actions performed in various modes; consequently, one speaks of a person repressing rigidly or denying euphorically.

3. Emotions, too, qualify as actions and modes of action. Thus, a person may be said to love or to hate, to love passionately or to hate inhibitedly, to speak lovingly or to judge hatefully. In action theory, the bodily concomitants of emotions are not taken as signs of cumulative and propulsive quantities that are logically distinct from, and temporally prior to, actions and that therefore require nominative and adjectival designation.

4. Wishing and believing are kinds of action. At least, they may be approached as interpretable actions in the psychoanalytic situation. In the philosophical literature it has been argued (e.g., by Davidson, 1963) that belief and desire are necessary constituents of intention, and that, to qualify as an action, an item of behavior must have at least one intentional description; from this it would follow that belief and desire cannot themselves be treated as actions. Nevertheless, in clinical analysis, one does often treat belief and desire as actions, as when one interprets *why* the analysand believes or desires something. On the assumption, then, that Davidson's analysis is not binding, the present line of argument will be continued. Thus, it may be said that, unconsciously, one wishes to perform particular actions or unconsciously believes oneself to be in specific infantile situations, and it may be asked why one wishes this or believes that. (I touch here on the concepts of fixation.)

5. When, consciously or unconsciously, one believes that the actions one is performing or wishes to perform are contradictory, irreconcilable, or paradoxical, one is acting conflictually. The same is true when one wishes that irreconcilable situations existed. It is the person who acts conflictually, not mental processes that do so.

6. The topographic qualities, so-called, are redescribable as modes of action. Thus, one may be said to wish *consciously, preconsciously,* or *unconsciously.* The mode unconsciously refers to what psychoanalysts are used to calling the dynamic unconscious: in this instance the word *unconsciously* is used to say that the person in question is managing to avoid representing

the matter consciously and is doing so for reasons and by methods which in principle are discoverable. These reasons, many of which are also denied recognition by the analysand, may include avoiding castigating oneself harshly or not alienating a person one loves or on whom one depends. The methods by which one accomplishes these more or less rigorous exclusions may be, for example, repressing or rationalizing. It remains to work out a full account in action language of all those consequential actions which are performed unconsciously, but that people do things unconsciously (in the "dynamic" sense) is one of the things we do want to say. (For an initial attempt of this sort, see my discussion of resistance in chapter 11 of *A New Language for Psychoanalysis*.)

7. That defensive measures themselves are engaged in unconsciously must be accounted for without getting into an infinite regress of actions performed unconsciously, that is, a regress in which each and every defensive action is the object of a further defensive action. In the chapter on resistance mentioned above, I tried to present just such an account; to summarize it would take too long, but it should at least be mentioned that Freud offered no satisfactory account of the dynamically unconscious status of the mechanisms of defense; he just made use of this observation, among others, to justify his formally replacing the topographic account of mental systems with the structural. Within metapsychology, purely psychoeconomic references to the deployment of countercathectic energies in defense do not deal adequately with the problem of infinite regress; nor do they offer a dynamic account of what is

to be explained. Unlike dynamic accounts, psychoeconomic accounts are empty of content—appropriately so. In the context of action language, it is, in
principle, possible to describe the actions by means of
which one represses, projects, etc. The description one
works out will center on two things: first, those actions,
such as separating, swallowing, defecating, and invad-
ing, that are unconsciously fantasized in connection
with each defensive measure and that give that measure
its meaning; and second, the faulty modes of representing self, others, and situations that are correlatives of
whatever is being fantasized.

8. Many types of reasons may be given for one
action, and the same reason may be given for a variety
of actions. (I touch here on the concepts of displacement, overdetermination, and multiple function.)

9. The formulation of the reason for an action states
what the action *is,* even though the form of that statement may be that of telling what the action is *for.* For
example, another way to say that the reason an analysand skipped an hour was to avoid a hostile confrontation with the analyst is to say that the analysand avoided
that hostile confrontation by skipping the hour. Then
one will be speaking of one event, not two, and so will
not be implying causal relations between reasons and
actions. At least one is under no obligation to use a
grammar that commits one to causal questions and
answers. Preconceptions favoring causal accounts generate a grammar that makes causal accounts seem im-
perative; mechanistic preconceptions are of this sort.
The grammar of action language puts things in a
different light. A corollary of the point that reasons

state what an action is, is that each reason used to explain an action implies another designation of the action itself. Consequently, if a second reason for skipping the analytic hour was to punish oneself for hating the analyst, it could be added that the analysand also punished himself or herself by skipping the hour.

These few illustrative remarks should make it plain that none of the complexity or subtlety of psychoanalytic understanding need be sacrificed by the adoption of noncausal action language. Everything interpretive that has been said or accepted in traditional psychoanalytic work may be translated into action language. It must be granted, however, that translation does necessarily involve at least some change of nuance. Nevertheless, it is my claim that the change in question is mainly a gain in systematic clarity through a reduction in one's theorizing of metaphoric allusiveness and mixed modes of discourse.

10. Actions may be described on any level of abstraction or with any degree of generality. Action language is not limited to being a micro-descriptive language; nor is it mere clinical description or simple-minded behavioristic description. For example, one may with equal warrant and consistency, though on decreasing levels of generality, say that a person is acting masochistically, enacting a rape fantasy, stimulating abusive and intrusive attitudes in others, or being irritatingly and teasingly coy. Being coy, in turn, is further reducible to one or another set of actions and modes of acting. On this basis action language lends itself to alternative, more or less concrete or abstract accounts of metapsychology's structural descriptions of mental processes and overt behaviors.

In action terms, these processes and behaviors may be characterized from the standpoint of their so-called id, ego, and superego aspects; they may be done, say, in a fashion that is uncompromisingly greedy and devouring or impetuously exhibitionistic (of the id type), guiltily reparative or self-punitive (of the superego type), responsibly judicious (of the ego type), or any combination. Nothing stands in the way of setting up abstract or general classes of actions to correspond to the familiar tripartite conception of mental structure, *if that is what is still wanted.* It is, however, no longer clear just what is wanted theoretically, in view of the underrationalized and uncoordinated proliferation of object-relations theories, self theories, lines-of-development theories, etc., with which we are confronted today. Incidentally, it can be shown that the referents of the tripartite scheme are necessarily actions and modes of action in the sense proposed here. These actions and modes are what the structural theory is about: the structural theory of psychoanalysis is a taxonomy of actions which has, however, been rendered so mechanistically and anthropomorphically that it seems like a framework for a psychodynamic explanation.

11. We come now, in points 11, 12, and 13, to the thorny problem of the relation of action language to bodily factors. Newborn infants do not perform actions; they manifest variable sensitivity to stimulation, reflexes, vegetative processes, and the like. Action, in the sense of things done for reasons or describable in terms of what a person desires and believes, is not part of the newborn's repertoire. The newborn and very young infant do develop conditioned responses as a primitive form of learning, and this learning, together with bio-

logical sensitivity and maturation, sets the stage for the dawn of human action. Characteristic constitutional sensorimotor thresholds and bodily modes of interacting with the mother, such as those described by child development researchers, are precursors of action as here defined.

Observers do, of course, confront a large gray area during the early months and years of development. This is the time when unstable, rudimentary, and global actions are sometimes—but only sometimes—describable. In this connection one may venture to say that Freud's instinct theory implicitly and unwarrantedly introduces action or psychological birth into the newborn's state of being. It does so through the concepts of *aim* of instinctual drives and *types* of psychic energy. It presents the newborn as a cognitively active person programmed to act for reasons, such as for the discharge of libidinal or aggressive drive-energy. The Kleinian psychoanalysts, going Freud one better, merely take this unwarranted step overtly and unrestrainedly (see, e.g., Segal, 1964). But the fact is that the prehistory of action is altogether obscure and the gray area still pretty obscure. Psychoanalysts ought to be able to live with this obscurity; one ought not press toward some absolutely continuous account of mental processes from day 1 on, through recourse to adultomorphic renditions of infant observation, speculative clinical reconstruction, and metapsychological preconceptions concerning instinctual aims and energies.

12. Psychoanalytic interpretation says why people do what they do. Though it takes account of happenings, it does not say what *makes* people do what they do, and

this is so even when such significant happenings as trauma are taken into account. Trauma is given meaning by its victim; analysts promote insight into the profoundly disturbing sense that the analysand has given to the traumatic event. Using action language, one does not work with ideas about forces, energies, and motives understood as propulsive entities. Action language is not based on the philosophical preconception that the psychological human being must be understood on the model of the machine, a machine being an apparatus that will not work in the absence of properly applied propulsive forces. The idea of propulsive psychological forces is a philosophical a priori, not a simple empirically observed fact. Metapsychology is based explicitly on this philosophical premise, and so, logically, it seeks the propulsive forces in the biological processes of the organism.

This is a very confused chapter in the history of psychoanalytic theory, and it is beyond the scope of this discussion to review the relevant critiques (see, e.g., Klein, 1976; Holt, 1976; Schafer, 1976). If, however, psychoanalysis is essentially an interpretive discipline, that is, a study of the goal-directed events that should be called actions and of the evolution of these actions in the life of the person undergoing clinical analysis, then it has no need to biologize its psychology. Nothing in the clinical analytic method leads to any conclusions about causal mind-body interactions, psychoeconomic closed systems, or overarching regulatory psychobiological principles such as repetition compulsion and life and death instincts. Far from being empirical conclusions, these are philosophical a prioris concerning the age-old mind-body problem, and at best they are dubious.

13. In working out any psychoanalytic account of the development and present status of psychic reality, one must, of course, assign a central place to the meanings the child has given to the actual conformations of human bodies, to actual bodily processes and changes, to actual bodily stimuli and bodily responsiveness to physical stimulation, and one must study closely the perpetuation of all these ascribed meanings. This requirement exists especially in connection with the erogenous zones, and most of all the mouth, anus, and genitalia. Important as it is that the stimuli emanating from these zones and the responsiveness of these zones to other stimuli seem to provide the material for major content of infantile experience, it is perhaps more important to consider what else they provide: these bodily factors may be seen as constituting the initially sensori-motor models or templates in terms of which experience begins to be constructed by the psychologically born infant. They provide, that is to say, the major infantile categories of understanding, such as entering into the breast, explosively expelling bad objects, hiding a secret penis, etc. Action language, far from entailing any disregard of Freud's *Three Essays on Sexuality* (1905a) and the "bodily ego" of *The Ego and the Id* (1923), establishes the sense of these contributions more clearly. Through action language, the familiar modes of body-oriented clinical interpretation, on which the entire idea of psychoanalysis should rest, are provided with a more logical, systematic basis. Too often, psychoanalysts confuse the subjective experience

of the body with biology, just as they confuse their attempts at a general psychology with their narrower sphere of data and competence.

14. Finally, I come to the all-important concept *experience*. The idea of action being presented here establishes experience as a construction of the individual. What the analysand reports introspectively as experience may be interpreted as one of his or her ways of saying something about what has been encountered in the world or in the body or what one has thought up. But, strictly speaking, that report in itself cannot be taken to show that anything is really the case in the sense that there is some final, unanalyzable, unredescribable account of reality being reached through inspection of experiental reports. There is no unanalyzable account of experience. To claim to verify a statement about the mind by looking into an independently given world of the mind is to lose sight of the fact that one can only be using one report to confirm another. When it comes to the analysis of experience, there are only pragmatic stopping points. The analysis of dreams is a good instance of this point. Analysts have always viewed experience as a creation that may be reflected upon, and that, in the reflective action, may be revised, developed further, and reinterpreted. The inner world of experience is a kind of telling, not a kind of place.

One must, however, take account of the fact that, in the course of their development and acquisition of language, people do learn and devise mentalistic categories that state or imply other conceptions of mind and experience. People get to say, for example, that they have a mind that has an inside and outside, divi-

sions in opposition to one another, and a mode of functioning, such as racing or blocking or discharging, that
it carries out independently of their own intentions.
Simultaneously, they say that they have a self or set of
selves, or an identity with or without boundaries, or a
set of irresistible compulsions. This is how they learn
to compose their experience, to tell themselves how
they are made. Further, people get to think of mental
performances or actions in terms of *can* and *can't* when
it is wrong logically, though understandable psychologically, to invoke the categories of ability and achievement. Logically, in the case of actions (not capacities)
they need only say what they do do and don't do and
what they agree to do and refuse to do.

It is not only that people get to take performance and
nonperformance as a measure of capacity or of success
and failure; they also think of facilitating and disruptive internal psychic forces, such as drives and prohibitions and inhibitions, acting on them for better or
worse, and, through disclaimers, they tell themselves
and others that they experience these influences passively, as events in which they are not implicated except as observers. In contrast, clinical psychoanalysts
have always interpreted these events as actions that
have been represented defensively, and they have regarded the modes of passive experience as constructions
amenable to interpretation rather than as the last word
on the subject under investigation. They have done
the same with reference to the presence or absence of
affects and their assumed discharge and with claims of
inner emptiness or deadness. They have analyzed them
whenever and to whatever extent it has seemed appro-

priate to do so and in whichever terms have seemed best suited to provoking insightful change. Unlike metapsychology, action language ensures that one honors this central fact of clinical life.

What is Distinctively Psychoanalytic about Psychoanalysis?

To answer this question first in the negative, metapsychology is not the defining feature. The positive answer emphasizes three points. First, psychoanalysis is the consistent attempt to understand the analysand's reports of private and public psychological events, especially in the transference and resistance, as actions that are susceptible to interpretation and reinterpretation. That is, these reports are considered open to multiple denomination and interrelation as actions, some of which underemphasize agency and others of which overemphasize it. Second, the psychoanalyst develops a focus on the archaic, more or less bodily and unconsciously maintained meanings of these actions. And third, the analyst states these meanings in terms of conflictual sexual and aggressive wishings and imaginings and in terms of those relevant infantile zones, substances, and situations which seem to threaten or enhance the self and others in relationship. In short, psychoanalysis is a set of rules for interpreting human action along certain lines in a certain context—that given uniquely in the psychoanalytic situation.

Many of these rules are still to be worked out. This is especially so in connection with higher-order abstractions. The nature of action language does not preclude

its further development. That development may—but
need not—lead to new ways of making, grouping, and
interrelating observations and interpretations, thereby
adding to the subtlety and effectiveness of the clinical
work that it is already possible to do.

REFERENCES

Bibring, E. 1936. The development and problems of the theory of the instincts. *Int. J. Psychoanal.* 50 : 293–308.

Davidson, O. 1963. Actions, reasons, and causes. *J. Philos.* 60 : 685–700.

Erikson, E. 1956. The problem of ego identity. *J. Amer. Psychoanal. Ass.* 4 : 56–121.

Fairbairn, W. R. D. 1952. *An object-relations theory of the personality.* New York: Basic Books, 1954.

Fenichel, O. 1941. *Problems of psychoanalytic technique.* Albany, N.Y.: Psychoanal. Quart. Press.

Freud, S. 1895. Project for a scientific psychology. In *The origins of psychoanalysis: letters to W. Fliess* (1887–1902). New York: Basic Books, 1954.

———. 1900. The interpretation of dreams. Stand. ed., vols. 4 & 5. London: Hogarth Press.

———. 1905a. Three essays on the theory of sexuality. Stand. ed., vol. 7. London: Hogarth Press.

———. 1905b. Jokes and their relation to the unconscious. Stand. ed., vol. 8. London: Hogarth Press.

———. 1909. Notes upon a case of obsessional neurosis. Stand. ed., vol. 10. London: Hogarth Press.

———. 1910–1912. Contributions to the psychology of love. Stand. ed., vol. 11. London: Hogarth Press.

———. 1911. Formulations on the two principles of mental functioning. Stand. ed., vol. 12. London: Hogarth Press.

———. 1915. The unconscious. Stand. ed., vol. 14. London: Hogarth Press.

———. 1920. Beyond the pleasure principle. Stand. ed., vol. 18. London: Hogarth Press.

———. 1923. The ego and the id. Stand. ed., vol. 19. London: Hogarth Press.

———. 1925a. Some additional notes on dream-interpretation as a whole. Stand. ed., vol. 19. London: Hogarth Press.

———. 1925b. Negation. Stand. ed., vol. 19. London: Hogarth Press.

———. 1926. Inhibitions, symptoms and anxiety. Stand. ed., vol. 20. London: Hogarth Press.

———. 1933. New introductory lectures on psycho-analysis. Stand. ed., vol. 22. London: Hogarth Press.

———. 1940. An outline of psycho-analysis. Stand. ed., vol. 23. London: Hogarth Press.

Gill, M. M. 1976. Metapsychology is not psychology. *Psychological Issues* 36 : 71–105.

Glover, E. 1955. *The technique of psycho-analysis.* New York: Int. Univ. Press.

Hartmann, H. 1939. *Ego psychology and the problem of adaptation.* New York: Int. Univ. Press, 1958.

Holt, R. R. 1976. Drive or wish? A reconsideration of the psychoanalytic theory of motivation. *Psychological Issues* 36 : 158–97.

Kernberg, O. 1975. *Borderline conditions and pathological narcissism.* New York: Jason Aronson.

Klein, G. S. 1976. *Psychoanalytic theory: an exploration of essentials.* New York: Int. Univ. Press.

Kohut, H. 1971. *The analysis of the self: a systematic approach to the psychoanalytic treatment of narcissistic personality disorders.* Monograph Series of the Psychoanalytic Study of the Child, No. 4. New York: Int. Univ. Press.

Kris, E. 1952. *Psychoanalytic explorations in art.* New York: Int. Univ. Press.

Laing, R. D. 1969. *The divided self: a study of sanity and madness.* New York: Pantheon Books.

Melden, A. I. 1961. *Free action.* New York: Humanities Press.

Ryle, G. 1949. *The concept of mind.* New York: Barnes and Noble, 1965.

Schafer, R. 1968. *Aspects of internalization.* New York: Int. Univ. Press.

————. 1974. Problems in Freud's psychology of women. *J. Amer. Psychoanal. Ass.* 22 : 459–85.

————. 1976. *A new language for psychoanalysis.* New York and London: Yale Univ. Press.

Segal, H. 1964. *Introduction to the work of Melanie Klein.* New York: Basic Books.

Thalberg, I. 1974. Freud's anatomies of the self. In *Freud: a collection of critical essays,* ed. R. Wollheim, 147–71. Garden City, N.Y.: Anchor Press/Doubleday.

Waelder, R. 1930. The principle of multiple function. *Psychoanal. Quart.* 15 (1936) : 45–62.

Winnicott, D. W. 1958. *Collected papers: through pediatrics to psychoanalysis.* New York: Basic Books.

Wittgenstein, L. 1942. *Lectures and conversations on aesthetics, psychology and religious belief,* ed. Cyril Barrett. Berkeley and Los Angeles: Univ. of California Press, 1972.

Woolf, V. 1929. *A room of one's own.* London: Hogarth.

INDEX

Acting out, 15, 16

Action: analysis as definition of rules in, 55; conditions and, 57; consistency of, 131–32; defense as, 21–22, 184; defining, 19–20; development and, 60–62; historical perspective through interpretation of, 20–21; inadequate self-control and, 73–77; language for psychoanalysis and, 7; life history as, 18–23; modes of, 19, 50–51; preparation of, 48–49; rule-following and, 60; self-control and, 71; thinking and speaking classified as, 48; use of term, 18–19; whole person and, 160–64

Action language in analysis, 8, 187–99

Alder, A., 66

Adolescence, 77–78

Aggressive conflicts, 9

Altruism, 20–21

Anal bodily categories, 9

Antilibidinal ego, 80

Attention cathexis, 47

Auden, W. H., 1, 27

Authentic self, 80

Automatisms, biological, 26

Autonomous ego functions, 75–76

Bibring, E., 82

Bisexuality, 164, 165

Bodily awareness, 9–10

Breast-phallus equation, 154–55

Castrating father, 23

Castration anxiety, 156

Cathexis, attention, 47

Causality, 56–58, 96

Childhood: defining self during, 9–10; seduction theory in, 170–71

Conditions: and action, 57

Conflict, 25; childhood defining of, 9; historical conditions and causality and, 58; resolution of, 100; self-control and, 92, 97–100

Conscious: as mental quality, 50; as mode of action, 189–90

Constructs: change in present world through, 24–25; of personal past, 8–13; of present subjective world, 14-18; subjective experience as, 23–24

Controlling self, 86–89

Countertransference, 115

Daughter-mother relationships, 155

Davidson, D., 189

Death instinct, 117, 129–30

Defense: as action, 184, 190–91; hatred as, 117; as personal activity, 21–22; self-control and, 97; self-love and self-hate and, 108

Determinism, 76

Development: action view of, 60–62; life history constructs and, 10–12

Differentiation: of self from mother, 156–58; sexual activity and, 146–47

Disclaimed action, 73–77

Displacement, 141

Divided self, 80

Dream analysis, 71–72

Drive tensions, 59–60

Dual-self theories, 80–84

Ego: action language and, 193; as bodily ego, 9–10; libidinal and